DEATH
At Sea

GRAF SPEE AND THE FLIGHT OF THE
GERMAN EAST ASIATIC NAVAL SQUADRON IN 1914

A NOVELISTIC HISTORY AND SENECAN TRAGEDY

ERIC DORN BROSE

Copyright © 2010 by Eric Dorn Brose

All rights reserved. No part of this manuscript may be
reproduced, stored in any retrieval system, or transmitted, in any
form or by any means, electronic, mechanical, photocopying,
recording, or otherwise, without the permission of the author.

ISBN: 1453738614
ISBN-13: 9781453738610

FOR MY WIFE, FAITH SUMNER, WHO NEEDS NO INSTRUCTION IN THE TRAGEDY OF WAR, AND WHO HAS HELPED ME SO MUCH TO WRITE THIS SAGA WITH THE NECESSARY DEPTH OF FEELING

•   •   •

AND FOR MY FATHER,
ROBERT WILLIAM BROSE, LIEUTENANT COMMANDER ABOARD THE USS *ABNER READ* DURING WORLD WAR TWO, WHO FIRST SPARKED MY INTEREST IN HISTORY WHEN HE GATHERED OUR FAMILY TOGETHER FOR SUNDAY EVENING EPISODES OF *VICTORY AT SEA* IN THE EARLY 1950s

THE SAGA UNFOLDS

I
DERBYSHIRE

The fourth Christmas of a seemingly endless war had come and gone. As the last days of 1917 faded drearily away, the bloody conflagration, history's worst, was about to drag into a fifth year. Intelligent people in all countries asked openly if anything meaningful would be left of the world when its "Great War" finally burned itself out, anything except the smoldering remains of a civilization in cinders.

One of these insightful skeptics sat in the British POW camp at Sutton Bonington, Derbyshire. His name and the name of his admiral were more familiar in England than the names of any other German naval officers with the possible exception of Alfred von Tirpitz, father of the German High Seas Fleet. The inmate was Karl von Müller, captain of the notorious light cruiser *Emden*. He had served with Graf Spee, commander of the awesome German East Asiatic Squadron, pride of the China station, and scourge of the British navy. Both Müller and Spee were legends in their own time—and beyond: in the 1930s two movies were made about their respective stories, one English, one German, and Adolf Hitler named his first battleship the *Graf Spee*.

The imprisoned skipper pulled out pen and paper, looked depressingly around his barebones cell, its only decoration a black wooden crucifix, and thought about what to write. He was a single man, so the most important family ties remained his parents back in Germany. He had written them often since first coming into British captivity on Malta in 1914, but no previous letter was as important as this one.

Would there be peace in 1918? Or would its arrival get pushed back into 1919? If peace finally came in that year, or the next, or the one after that, could a war which had already killed eight million and badly maimed many millions more, actually end abruptly? Or would it, like the aftershocks of a cataclysmic earthquake, rain damage and destruction on humankind for years or maybe decades after the "peace" treaties?

It was shocking to think about, but perhaps the Great War had already maimed the entire twentieth century. Whichever country came out a loser would want revenge some day—the next war could be worse, much worse, than this one. Worse still, communists had just come to power in Russia. They would hold onto their power tenaciously and wage war against all non-communist countries, which surely meant perpetual trouble. There would be more war—and peace would only be a sort of war: a fearful, apprehensive waiting for war. A century full of hot war, cold war, and probably terrorism too.

Müller began to write. From time to time he emphatically underlined certain words. There was a very serious look about him which did not change as his thoughts spilled out onto paper:

2

"Sutton Bonington   December 30th 1917

I hope that my letters continue to make it through the blockade, loving parents. I am still in British captivity. There is talk of sending me to Holland in some sort of prisoner exchange to treat my malaria, which has flared up again, but so far nothing. Like the survivors of our noble East Asiatic Squadron back in Malta I long to see Germany again. What I would not give to be back with you in our beautiful Harz Mountain Heimat. For now there remains the sole consolation that I— and every last one of us—served the Fatherland with honor.

Honor—it seems that there is less of it in the world these days. Since my capture three years ago several greedy publishers have urged me to write an inside account of the operations of the East Asiatic Squadron. I am very proud of the war record of SMS Emden. My cruiser threw a scare into the heart of the British Empire that will not soon be forgotten. And my admiral inflicted one of the worst defeats on the Royal Navy in its entire history. But I cannot accept these publication offers, and I shall <u>never</u> accept them. Were I to publish our story, I would regard myself as arrogant, and I should not be able to escape the feeling that I was coining money from the blood of my comrades.

But perhaps some good may come of it if I write a private memoir <u>for you</u>, dear mother and father. At the very least, by my telling, I may ameliorate the pain, the remorse, <u>and the guilt</u> that I feel every day and every night.

But there's something more important. You must know that since childhood I have always aimed to please you, to make you proud of me. So it is with some misgiving and trepidation that I shall try in this memoir to correct some of the false impressions that so many people have about war in modern times. I also want you to learn something about it, and then tell others, so that they may also learn. After all, are not those who know obliged to tell?

Let me be perfectly clear about this, my parents. War, especially the Great War that broke upon our troubled world that summer of 1914 like a terrible squall, is not glorious—it is, rather, tragedy writ large. But, you will say, there are all of the good things: duty, honor, country, camaraderie, and at times mercy. While this is certainly true, my war was also about extremely hard-fought victories, about terrible destruction, about agonizing, horrific death. And for one side or the other it was clear from the outset that it would most certainly also be about anguishing defeat.

Yes, there are some good things about war, but mostly it is all the work of the devil. A whole generation is being decimated. A century may pass and the world we knew will not have returned. Things were far from perfect, but at least there was peace. That world is gone—gone forever.

Whatever you take from our story, however, do not call us heroes. We performed no special deeds, but only did our duty."

II
COLOMBO

I arrived in Colombo harbor, Ceylon, in the autumn of 1914. The English placed me aboard the yellow-funneled *Orvieto* of the Orient Line, just one of thirty-eight ships convoying 28,000 Australian and New Zealander troops of the ANZAC corps to Suez for defense of the canal against Germany's ally, the Turks. A few days after we arrived I was taken by the *Orvieto*'s steam launch over to the armored cruiser HMS *Hampshire*, soon to be the new flagship of the ANZAC convoy.

As the little transport maneuvered among the scores of ships in the harbor, thousands of spectators crowded the deck railings to catch a glimpse of, or flash their cameras at, me, the enemy, the man the Royal Navy had hunted for many months. This was the final humiliation. My ship was destroyed, so many of my men were dead, and now I was put on public display before an alien people, paraded in chains like a beaten Hun warrior in a Roman triumph. An end to this could not come soon enough. At last I was taken aboard and escorted to the *Hampshire*'s wardroom, where the good captain of this ship received me.

•   •   •

Karl von Müller was deeply patriotic. The family's men on his father's side had been army officers many generations back, while on the maternal side his uncle was a famous nationalist politician who played an active role in the founding of the German Empire in 1871.

Karl von Müller: "Do not call us heroes"
(Hohenzollern, *Emden*)

Born two years later, Müller became a naval cadet in 1891. With his schooling painstakingly and conscientiously finished, he rose rapidly through the ranks, receiving his first three captain's stripes in 1908. Five years later the new forty-year old skipper of *SMS Emden* saw action against Chinese rebels on the Yangtze River, for which he was awarded the Imperial Crown Order, Third Class with Swords, and given his fourth stripe.

Müller was almost pathologically determined to succeed. He yearned to accomplish something that would equal or perhaps exceed the accomplishments of his family forebears. That he had chosen to do this in the navy and not the more prestigious German army was one sign of the independent streak in his personality, a trait reinforced by the great measure of confidence that he had in himself. But the young captain was also conflicted, for, vying with the confidence that he was right, and would succeed, was a nagging, haunting fear that he could fail. These fears made him think twice as hard, however, about how to succeed—he thought things through more than most men.

Whatever happened in the navy, whatever he did or did not achieve, there was one unforgivable failing he swore he would avoid: doing anything to dishonor the family and the Fatherland. This meant waging war as a gentleman, as a nobleman, and as a man of honor. Defeated enemies would receive quarter and civilians would be spared the horrors of war. But was there room in the Great War of 1914-1918 for a man of Müller's ilk? Was it perhaps not a little naïve of him to think that he could succeed in a world as deeply troubled as that which rushed suicidally to arms in August 1914?

· · ·

"Welcome aboard," said the saluting British skipper, dressed in clean regulation whites. "I trust you have been treated well since our talk under sadder circumstances two days ago." He gestured toward alcoholic beverages set out on the wardroom table and offered highly coveted English cigarettes from a golden cigarette box.

"Today's circumstances are no less sad for me, Captain Grant," replied the German, still clearly angry, his uniform bearing the unmistakable yellowy cordite stains of recent combat, "but thank you, a whisky and soda would be greatly appreciated. And, as you know, we've gotten very accustomed in recent months to your highly 'prized' cigarettes," said with just a pinch of pride and a dash of contempt.

"Ah yes, I know—Australia has no cigarettes because they all ended up on the *Emden!*" said Grant as he fixed the drinks. He lit both smokes and motioned that they be seated.

Turning more serious, Grant continued with the wartime proprieties. "The circumstances are now sad for the Royal Navy too, captain. I'm afraid I have the advantage of news that may not have reached you yet of the smashing victory of your Admiral Spee and the East Asiatic Squadron."

As Grant sadly explained what he knew, Müller's thoughts raced ahead—he could barely listen—to visions of a victory at sea that had only been thought likely or possible by a few in the Imperial German Navy before the war. After feeling humiliated just minutes earlier, he could now feel better about something.

Grant paused, respectful of both Spee and of the British dead. "But I can assure you that Graf Spee is now being pursued by his avengers."

"I'm quite sure of that." Müller paused. "I know the men of the Royal Navy met their deaths bravely. My condolences." He paused again. "The fortunes of war are never *always* positive, captain," observed the German, eyes narrowing without saying the obvious, that he knew this all too well. "But war is war. We do our duty," he proclaimed, his head turning proudly up to one side while he blew smoke, cigarette held between thumb and forefinger in the style of German nobility.

Grant nodded acceptance of Müller's accurate words, but pensively and wistfully said nothing, as if thinking about different times.

"Do you remember 1913 on the Yangtze, Captain Müller? In that day—was it only last year?—we fought on the same side, two mighty empires defending their common imperial interests in China. I can assure you that no one on our side cherished what we went through these last few months. In fact I dreaded the thought of *Hampshire* sighting *Emden* as we looked throughout the whole bloody Indian Ocean for you!"

"And I need not say to you, captain, that almost no one in the German East Asiatic gave more than a passing thought to the possibility, the *crazy* notion, that we would some day be fighting our courageous brother sailors of the Royal Navy. Why, it was only six months ago that HMS *Minotaur* visited Tsingtao!"

Now it was Müller's turn to think for a moment, smiling, about different times. "Yes, our beautiful Tsingtao."

Then he straightened up abruptly. "The Japanese must have captured it by now?"

"Yes, a few weeks ago, with our help."

"Our lovely Tsingtao Japanese? Hard to think about that ... hard ..." he whispered in believing disbelief.

Now Grant's eyes narrowed: "But, as you said, war is war, and its fortunes are never *always* positive."

Already getting awkward, the brief visit was over.

III
TSINGTAO

The new foliage of springtime sparkled in our far-away colony of Tsingtao. Summer would come soon. Under a blue, almost cloudless sky, for as far as one could see, unfolded a panorama more beautiful than any canvas in a museum: lush green hills, red-roofed houses, the jagged Chinese mountains, the tranquil bay, and the surging ocean. On board steamers from every European nation cranes rattled incessantly day and night. Goods came and went, Chinese peddlers with overloaded wheelbarrows jostled each other on the road into town, and all around one heard the sounds and witnessed the animation of business.[1]

There was also much hustle and bustle on the ships of the East Asiatic, for the annual relief from the Fatherland of half the crews of the squadron was only days away. The much-anticipated day that once a year gave our duty on the China station fresh life came on June 2nd when the ocean liner *Patricia* entered the harbor with 1,600 sailors.

Greeted on all sides with cheers, she dropped anchor, and within a few hours each contingent of replacements had lined up on the dock, sea bags on

1   From Pochhammer, *Before Jutland*. See my methodological Afterword.

shoulders, next to the vessel which was to be their home for the next two years. Their eyes wandered curiously along the grey hulls, and turned up, full of wonder, at the masts, funnels, and big guns, all of which seemed so very large at such close quarters. Soon the new men were all on the gangways coming aboard.

A few days later it was the turn of those being relieved to board the *Patricia*, bound back to Germany. When the hour of departure approached our homeward-bound comrades on the *Patricia* crowded the decks closest to shore and filled the rigging, while on the dock below crowds gathered from the ships' crews and the colony to shout a last farewell. Bands on board and on shore exchanged rousing march tunes, trying to impose notes of gaiety to what was, after all, a sad and serious moment. At 1100 hours ropes were cast away and the anchor lifted. Three loud blasts from the liner's fog horn demanded the right of way. As the huge ship moved slowly backward, and then turned about in the harbor, people cheered and hats waved all around.

On June 13th HMS *Minotaur* steamed through the bay and into the harbor of Tsingtao for an official visit. The big ship's Union Jack fluttered in the wind as she made the approach to docking. Our band played "Rule Britannia" out of courtesy and respect. English sailors threw hawsers to German sailors on the peer. Every German chest puffed with pride as we made ready to host the most powerful navy in the world.

Minotaur was the flagship of the British Far Eastern Fleet, out of Hong Kong, under the command of Admiral Thomas Jerram. She had been built as an answer to my squadron's armored heavy cruisers, *Scharnhorst* and *Gneisenau*. She was a little bigger and faster and carried slightly heavier guns, so we were all curious to see her, but as strange as this may seem, almost no one wondered about the outcome of a naval battle because peace had reigned for decades in Europe. We were thinking, rather, that this visit was going to be a grand time.

And it was. One of the highlights of the many social events and excursions we had planned for the entertainment of our English guests was the open house that my admiral, Graf Maximilian von Spee, hosted on the stern deck of *Scharnhorst*. Beneath the aft gun turret was spread every delicacy we could assemble with ample provisions of good German beer and Rhenish wine. Spee was proud to host this function with his sons, Otto and Heinrich, both officers in the squadron, standing to each side.

•   •   •

The family of Müller's admiral, Maximilian Johannes Maria Hubertus, Graf von Spee, traced its noble lineage back to the 12th Century. Count von Spee was fifty-three years old and had served in the Imperial German Navy since joining it as a sixteen-year-old cadet in 1877. A lieutenant commander by 1897, he began a rapid ascent in the entourage of his mentor, Prince Heinrich, the Kaiser's younger brother, serving under him with the Second Fleet Division that reinforced Tsingtao in 1898, and, again under the Prince, as a commander and first officer of battleship *Brandenburg* during the suppression of the Boxer Rebellion in China in 1900.

Graf Spee with Heinrich (left) and Otto (right) in 1912
(Kirchoff, *Maximiliam Graf von Spee*)

He had advanced by 1905 to the rank of captain of the refurbished *Wittelsbach*, one of four battleships in the "Brandenburg Squadron," the spearhead of the High Seas (i.e. North Sea) Fleet. These capital ships quickly became obsolete, however, when the British began to produce the bigger, faster "Dreadnought" class of battleships the following year. In 1908 Commodore von Spee became chief of staff of the home fleet under its chief, Prince Heinrich, as Germany embarked on its own dreadnought/battle cruiser revolution. In late 1912 Graf Spee, by then rear admiral, was given command of the East Asiatic Squadron and promoted to vice-admiral, thereby returning to the overseas duties that had been the hallmark of his naval career.

A deeply religious Catholic and dyed-in-the-wool conservative, Spee thought women should marry within their class and race, if not within their church—his wife, forty seven year-old Margarete von Spee, née Freiin von der Osten-Sacken, was Lutheran. He disapproved of modern dances like the tango, disliked pompous official functions, ate, drank, and smoked in strict moderation, and brooked no indiscipline, insubordination, or subversiveness of any sort. His appearance—tall and broad-shouldered with an erect posture, looking, as one officer recalled, like he had swallowed a broomstick—mirrored exactly his authoritarian personality. He was usually practical and pragmatic enough to discuss issues and have others vet his ideas and plans, but once he made a decision, that was that—one had to obey. Even if doubt and anxiety crept into his own thoughts—as they often did with this fatalistic seaman—one had to obey fate.

• • •

Besides the shipboard open house we had planned all manner of friendly competition in the spirit of the brotherhood of the sea. There was rowing, boxing, gymnastics, relay races and high jumping at our athletic field, even gunnery target shoots between crews in the bay, at which the fast white *Emden*, dubbed by sailors of all nations on the China station "The Swan of the East," excelled. The entire squadron was filled with crack gunners too—we were the best in the world, even better than our home fleet, which itself had no world equal in gunnery.

The main event, however, was unquestionably the soccer match, which was tied 2-2 at the end of regulation play before the Brits found their *élan vital* in the overtime period, scoring three goals to our none as every German in attendance buried head in hands. But we found our vital national energy in the tug of war with the mooring rope. When the gun shot our sailors used a surprising technique: they picked up the hawser, turned to the rear, locked it over their shoulders, and started walking, tugging the entire British team across the line, all this to the roars of Germans watching.

On the third day of the English visit something quite remarkable happened—it seemed like nothing at the time, but now I am drawn back to it. All of the senior German officers, including Graf Spee, were having a luncheon at our favorite restaurant, the Dachsal. With us was Julius Lauterbach, a big, burly, heavy-drinking captain of a German mail steamer. He was also a member of the naval reserve and proudly sported a saber scar on his left cheek, a badge of honor earned during rowdy former days. Lauterbach had a lady friend in every port between Suez and Tsingtao, or so he claimed. He also fancied himself quite the stage performer, often reciting lines for us he had memorized from Shakespeare and other poets and playwrights. But he did know every square inch of the Indian Ocean and Western Pacific like the back of his hand. The eccentric fellow had recently had an interesting conversation with a Dutch missionary.

•   •   •

"You're far too heavy, Lauterbach," said Hans Pochhammer, first officer of SMS *Gneisenau*. "You need to lose fifty pounds."

"I weigh 255 pounds, Pochhammer, and don't intend to lose a single one of them!" he exclaimed before taking a gulp and slamming his beer stein on the table and wiping the foam off his mouth to the noticeable disapproval of the admiral.

"Now gentlemen let me have your attention for a moment," Lauterbach said. The others exchanged skeptical glances as if they did not take him seriously.

"No, seriously, let me tell you what I heard the other day from a Dutch clergyman returning from home leave. He said that war is on everyone's lips in Europe. Then his train on the Trans-Siberian Railroad was repeatedly sidetracked as Russian troop trains roared west—west, gentlemen, to the German border! I've asked to be put on active duty, for this summer there will be a war!"

The others laughed with disbelieving, mildly respectful restraint. Only the *Emden*'s first officer, Helmuth von Mücke, long a fervent believer that war, even with England, would come, did not laugh.

Privately, Graf Spee did not believe in the possibility of peace with England any more than Mücke. The prospect worried him, in fact, for admiralty had planned to reinforce the East Asiatic with a new flagship, SMS

Moltke, a battle cruiser carrying big guns like a dreadnought only much faster due to thinner armor plate, but her deployment had been postponed. Keeping his worries to himself, however, the admiral decided to poke some fun of his own at the big man.

"You drink too much, Lauterbach," he said smiling. "Drinking has warped your judgment. Why I've just returned from hunting with Admiral Jerram, and we were shooting at the tripe, not at each other!"

Julius Lauterbach: The others did not take him seriously
(Thomas, *Lauterbach*)

The table broke out in roaring laughter. Even Mücke managed to smile a little. Seeing this, Lauterbach realized his apparent silliness, and then joined his comrades in laughter.

But, graciously, Graf Spee asked the reservist a question: "Which of my ships would you like to board, whether or not we all get into a scrap, Lauterbach?"

Without a moment's hesitation, Lauterbach, who knew many of the officers of the *Emden*, including its skipper, answered: "*Emden!*"

· · ·

My first officer, Helmuth von Mücke, had only recently been promoted to Lieutenant Commander and his new post, his predecessor having shipped out on the *Patricia*. I respected his spit and polish approach to discipline and the proper training of the crew, but was not particularly close to him personally. This was due to Mücke's intense interest in—his near monomania for—politics, which I felt was unbecoming of a nobleman and an unwanted distraction from technical naval matters. My fiery first officer spent seemingly every spare moment reading about politics and foreign affairs in the newspapers, and then subjected everybody within earshot to a lecture. I was put off by this know-it-all-ism, this "*Besserwisserei*," as we say.

Mücke's favorite hobby horse was hatred for England, which by his telling had no honor: a nation of merchants who cheated and stole, a nation that betrayed and back-stabbed, a nation that could not be trusted. To Mücke the English were, with the Jews, the conspiratorial natural enemy of the Germans. Mücke would obviously be fearless in battle, but his ranting concerned me. Would he somehow bring us dishonor or hamper our mission?

•   •   •

Almost none among us wanted *Minotaur* to steam away on June 16th. The mood was gay and optimistic. Many on both sides had made bold assertions and given assurances that, despite the tensions ratcheting up in Europe, brother would never fight brother.

IV
WAR

On June 29th, after Graf Spee and most of the squadron had left port to show the flag amidst our Pacific island colonies, electrifying news pulsed into our wireless station. A day earlier Serbian terrorists had assassinated the heir to the throne of the Austro-Hungarian Empire, Francis Ferdinand, in Sarajevo, Bosnia. Terrorism had come to a world that would never be free of terrorism.

This murder heightened the probability of war in continental Europe. It took no diplomatic genius to predict what *might* happen, for there had been many dress rehearsals in recent years. Austria-Hungary, long regarding the Serbs as racial enemies, would want to punish Serbia with the sword. Russia would swarm into the fray to protect its Slavic brethren in Serbia from eradication by Germanic enemies in the north. Germany, long treaty-bound to Austria-Hungary, would never tolerate Russian annihilation of an ethnic friend and ally—Germany would enter the fight against Russia—but this also meant war against France, long the ally of Russia. Many of us assumed that Britain would remain neutral, but others, especially Mücke, said no, she would join Russia and France. In a powder flash, all of Europe might explode, unless, that is, the diplomats found a way out of the crisis. In all previous crises, in fact, the diplomats had found ways to keep the peace. Why could they not again?

Even when Graf Spee canceled *Emden*'s scheduled cruise to Shanghai due to the possibility of war, most of us in Tsingtao went about our normal duties and were not especially alarmed. That was July 8th. There also seemed little reason to worry about a seemingly incredible message from the Admiralty in Berlin on the 11th mentioning the anti-German leanings of Britain.

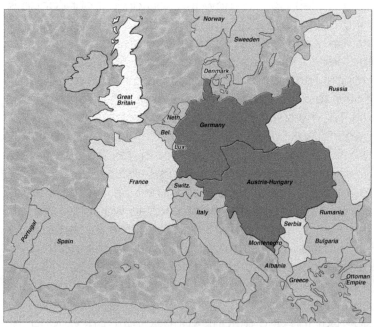

EUROPE IN AUGUST 1914
(Peter Groesbeck)

But as July drew to a close the crisis in Europe careened out of control. Austria declared war on

Serbia, Russian mobilized its army, then Germany, then France. The diplomats, exhausted by previous crises, had failed. On July 29th *Emden* received orders from Admiralty to rejoin the East Asiatic Squadron, which was still scattered all over the Pacific, one of our light cruisers, SMS *Leipzig*, patrolling off California and Mexico, but Graf Spee countermanded this, ordering our ship to do what we could to disrupt enemy commerce in the Far East and to be on the lookout for Russian and French warships—both were soon at war with Germany. We prepared *Emden* for war.

The last thing I wanted was to be trapped in Tsingtao by enemy ships stationed in nearby waters—"Copenhagened" like the Danish ships long ago destroyed in harbor by the English—but after years of peacetime duty there was a lot of work to do—and not much time to do it. Civilian clothes no longer needed and all of the extra comforts officers and men had brought into their quarters had to be removed. Wood panels, upholstered chairs, carpets, and curtains—all that could burn or splinter in battle had to be stripped. Live warheads had to replace the blanks on the 17.5-inch torpedoes. A full complement of live shells had to be loaded from ammunition depots for our ten 4.1-inch guns. Our triple expansion steam engines and boilers had to be thoroughly cleaned and maintenanced. And always coal, coal, and more coal had to be taken laboriously on board.

Finally at 1900 hours on July 31st we put to sea.

• • •

Müller and his crew had been almost a week at sea by August 5th. They cruised the Tsushima Straits between Korea and Japan, having captured a Russian merchantman, *Emden*'s first prize. Lauterbach, who had indeed been put on active duty, commanded her astern to port.

That evening the captain and his officers finished their dinner, and then gathered on the quarterdeck for cigarettes and cigars. Five minutes later, as they relaxed and chatted a while, the ship's adjutant, Lieutenant von Guérard, raced out of the radio room toward the officers. Only twenty-one years old, amiable, affable, and baby-faced, Guérard was the one officer who was closest to the captain—his favorite, so to speak.

Spotting Müller, the young officer ran up to him. "This could be important, sir. Admiralty has wired: 'enigma.' "

The captain's expression changed instantly from relaxed to all-business. "What was that you said?"

"One word, sir: 'enigma.' "

For a long moment there was total silence. Finally the captain turned to the others: "Gentlemen, your attention please. England, too, has declared war on Germany … Come with me, Mücke."

They went back to the wardroom, which was almost cleared. They waited for the stewards to finish clearing the table. When the room was empty the captain began to speak, but, still a little taken aback, paused, which gave the first officer an opportunity to speak his piece.

SMS *Emden:* The Swan of the East
(Mücke, *Emden*)

"I always said, even though no one wanted to listen, that the English could not be trusted."

"This is no time for I-told-you-so," came the curt reply. "Britain's declaration of belligerency creates an altogether different situation for us. The squadron might possibly be able to defeat the Russian cruisers, the French cruisers, and even the British cruisers, assuming the enemy did not concentrate all of his ships against ours—but fighting the many battleships and battle cruisers of the Japanese, too, would be suicide. They are Britain's ally and will declare war against us. Set course for Tsingtao. We must load coal and find Graf Spee."

As the first officer left the wardroom to execute his orders, the captain leaned on the bulkhead and peered through a porthole at the Straits. He thought to himself, grimacing: "So, Admiralty was right after all … But how could our leaders have allowed policy to so deteriorate beyond reason to the point where mighty Britain would go to war against us?! Are they mad? … Or was Mücke right all along, that England was only waiting for an opportunity to stab us in the back? … Ah well, it makes little difference now. We can't dream about what might have been. We have to face the facts, for grim facts will soon be facing us … And if I know the admiral, he also wants to exit these waters, but only to set sail for Germany to do battle in the North Sea. We'll never make it."

V
PAGAN

On August 12th we sighted volcanic Pagan Island, northernmost of the German Marianas, the spot Graf Spee had chosen for the squadron to rendezvous. As the ships drew closer and closer a more detailed and colorful picture came into focus. The crews had not been told our destination, but all recognized Pagan's two distinctive volcano crowns, perpetually shrouded in smoke, its strange rock formations and intimidating cliffs, coconut palms, mangrove bushes, and tropical vegetation. As the ships neared the entrance to the bay, still blocked from view off the portside by a huge cliff, a smaller gunboat rounded the cape, signaled *Emden* by semaphore, and reversed course back around the bend: she would guide us to our anchorage.

We steered into the bay, where an impressive, overpowering panorama opened before us against the backdrop of tropical Pagan. The men had not seen their comrades since June and thus were elated at the still distant sight to port of light cruiser *Nürnberg* and the bigger *Gneisenau*, separated by several hundred yards, and to starboard the flagship, *Scharnhorst*.

At the sight of *Emden* loud cheers and hurrahs went up from the warships of the German East Asiatic Squadron, for a report—now obviously false—had been received of our sinking by a larger Russian cruiser. Since leaving Tsingtao we had been accompanied by *Prince Eitel Friedrich*, a German steamer that had been converted to an auxiliary cruiser and now boasted its own complement of eight 4.1-inch guns. Seven steamers were also moored all over the bay, including Lauterbach's old ship, *Staatssekretaer Kraetke*. They would serve as squadron colliers. *Emden*'s collier, *Markomannia*, was due to arrive in the morning.

SMS *Scharnhorst*: Showing the flag in the Pacific
(Pochhammer, *Graf Spee's letzte Fahrt*)

Almost immediately after dropping anchor I boarded *Emden*'s steam launch and went across the bay to *Scharnhorst*. Graf Spee wanted me to report on our exploits and the situation in Tsingtao. Knowing me as he did, the admiral expected that I would also want to discuss the squadron's next moves.

• • •

Müller had very bold views on naval tactics and strategy. He had served for two years with the founder of the German fleet, Admiral Alfred von Tirpitz, in the Navy Ministry in Berlin. It was there that he honed his arguments *against* using the fleet, as Tirpitz intended, to gain diplomatic leverage over the British, and perhaps even defeat the mighty Royal Navy—a great, titanic battle that also tempted Graf Spee. Rather, Müller had become an adherent of *guerre de course*, the concept of striking blows at the commerce of enemy nations, which was less likely to succeed against Britain, the leading maritime nation in the world bar none in 1914, but would clearly be more effective against Germany's weaker naval foes on the continent, France and Russia. They would be blockaded and their merchant ships swept from the world's oceans. It was for this reason that he applied for, and received, the captaincy of his fast and formidable light cruiser. When war came in 1914, however, Britain was unexpectedly on the other side. Müller came to the conclusion, natural for him, that whatever the odds commerce warfare against the British Empire should commence as soon as possible.

Given Graf Spee's traditionalist nature, it was no coincidence that his views on tactics and strategy were more conservative. A fleet or squadron could only project its power in the waters it ventured into with superior numbers, superior technology, and superior gunnery—twice the East Asiatic had won the Kaiser's Cup for the best marksmanship in the entire Imperial German Navy. Unless completely outclassed by enemy dreadnought battleships or battle cruisers, the squadron's mission was to engage and destroy the enemy. Accepting the fact that he lived in modern times, Graf Spee realized that victory at sea also meant dealing a blow to enemy commerce in the region one would control after a victorious sea battle—the one would follow the other—but he did not dwell on the commercial side of naval affairs, nor did he think it a very honorable aspect of war.

• • •

Müller was piped aboard *Scharnhorst* and taken to his admiral's resplendent day suite. Spee sat on one side of a long conference table, studying charts and the latest dispatches from Berlin. To his left, occupying the entire wall, hung an ornate colored map of the world that stretched from East Africa on the far left, through the Indian Ocean and the Pacific Ocean, and across the Americas and the Atlantic Ocean to West Africa on the far right. After the traditional round of drinks, Spee asked *Emden*'s skipper to report.

After doing so Müller lingered and finally screwed up the courage to pursue his agenda.

"By your leave, sir, may I take a few more minutes of the admiral's time?"

"But of course Müller. What's on your mind? Wondering what's on mine?" he said with a sour, all-knowing smile.

"Why yes, sir, that's it exactly. How can the squadron best serve Kaiser and country?"

"Just between us, our four eyes, for now, ja?"

"Ja, ja, of course."

"I've asked all ships' captains to a briefing on this matter tomorrow at 0900. I'll issue orders for the squadron after hearing all points of view, but certain things are obvious already now."

"Britain's entry to the war," he continued, "and the likely declaration of war by Japan totally rule out a return to Tsingtao, where we would be bottled up and destroyed, or remaining in the Western Pacific, where we would meet the same end. If the squadron is to be reunited, *giving us some strength in numbers* ..."

Graf Spee stopped for a moment for a breath.

"If we are to *maximize our strength*, that means sailing east. Light cruiser *Leipzig* is patrolling off the California coast," he said gesturing to the center of his wall map. "We could rendezvous, perhaps at Easter Island."

When Spee mentioned strength in numbers and paused, Müller thought: "The British will send their big fast battle cruisers, and that will be that—mass death at sea without striking a blow against the enemy of the Fatherland." When Spee finished, the junior man took a second to consider which words to choose: "He is such a traditional man of the sea, looking only for battle. But our cruisers can best be deployed as surface raiders against merchant ships. How can I convince him?"

31

"Sir, you know my views on *guerre de course*. All of our ships are faster than any merchant vessel."

Pointing to the left side of the map, he continued.

"Perhaps we should consider splitting up the squadron and slipping into the Indian Ocean and operating independently as surface raiders, as corsairs. Using the Dutch East Indies as a haven and supply of coal, seizing the rest of our coal from British and neutral merchantmen in the Indian Ocean, we can operate indefinitely and strike a lethal economic blow against the enemy."

He stopped for a second, and as he did Spee thought indignantly: "I am *not* a pirate!"

Müller continued. "After we take one prize ship after another, one hundred or more, the Indian Ocean, that English lake, will be swept clean of commerce and troop convoys from Australia, New Zealand, and India. Their war effort will be badly hurt, and, worse for them, the Indians will surely seize the opportunity to rise up against their hated English overlords. They tried it in 1857 and will try it again. They'll have to remove soldiers from Europe to protect their empire."

He paused again as Spee thought even more indignantly: "I am *not* a revolutionary!"

Emden's skipper concluded: "They may catch up with us sooner or later, but in the meantime half of the British fleet, including battle cruisers and dreadnoughts, will be chasing us. At home, Admiralty will finally have the superior odds it needs to defeat the remainder of the British Grand Fleet in the North Sea and break the anticipated British blockade of Germany. If we can't break that blockade Britain will surely strangle the Fatherland to death! We won't have food—and we won't have the raw materials that Germany lacks for production of munitions! We must break their blockade—or we die!"

Spee drummed his fingers impatiently as Müller finished. After a moment Spee's look of slight disgust disappeared as he gathered himself together, masking his feelings.

"Let's assume our efforts net a hundred merchant ships—but the English have three thousand steamers, so it doesn't seem to me a wise expenditure of scarce German overseas naval resources." Contented that he had won this bridge hand—as he usually did—the admiral reapplied his sour, all-knowing smile.

"Sir, I referred to the Indian Ocean as an English lake for a good reason. From the east coast of Africa, over Arabia and India and Malaysia, including Singapore, to Australia and New Zealand, they rule, but if we seize the initiative and begin to sink and capture ships, steamer captains will panic and stay cowardly in port. Sinking or taking a hundred ships will leave many hundreds more, perhaps a thousand more, economically useless at anchor."

Graf Spee, still wryly smiling somewhat politely in noble fashion, played his next bridge hand.

"You're assuming the war will last long enough for their blockade, and our reverse pirate blockade, to be effective. But if our army wins by winter, what then? Britain will lose a few infantry divisions and keep their Grand Fleet in tact for the next war. If the East Asiatic can break successfully for South America, however, and if Admiralty detaches a few capital ships for overseas operations, we could unite with them, defeat whatever the English send against us, sail for home, and then crash through their naval cordon. There is still time to assist the main fleet in destroying perfidious Albion and eliminating the last check to German world power."

Müller did not look convinced, but he had to choose his words carefully: "Do you believe that our two armored heavy cruisers will make a difference against the massive English navy?"

"Yes I do. Their blockade will wear on ships constantly at sea, forcing them to put into port for maintenance. Attrition of this sort will make the numbers of capital ships on each side in battle closer than you'd think. So yes, our big cruisers *will* make a difference."

Then, nodding politely, and showing every sign of having nixed Müller's objectionable scheme, Graf Spee terminated the meeting: "Yes, much is at stake as we consider our options. Until tomorrow then?"

Müller saluted and left.

•   •   •

As he returned to *Emden*, dusk settling over the bay, the captain spotted Lauterbach approaching from the opposite direction in another launch. "If Spee decides to unleash us on British commerce," mused Müller, "Lauterbach will be the perfect man to have along, the perfect prize officer. He knows the waters and harbors better than I, as a merchant captain he knows how to identify cargoes, he can command any captured prize ship we take along with us, and he is the ideal personality for consoling distraught captains whose prize ships we sink. He's not career navy, but he knows our ways ... Wait, what's this?"

As Müller's launch pulled alongside *Emden*, Lauterbach let his captain board first, but the other vessel was close enough for Müller to see Lauterbach's cargo: stacks of books, enough cigarettes for the entire crew, numerous fully stocked wine racks, and perhaps a dozen cases of beer and whisky. Lauterbach had returned from his old ship with the entire contents of the captain's cabin. There were even two upholstered chairs.

He cast an angry glance at the big man: "Those overstuffed chairs will burn nicely in our boilers, Lauterbach. We'll break 25 knots. That is if you don't capsize first."

Caught red-handed, Lauterbach shrugged his shoulders, then, saluting, said: "You're quite right sir."

"And I see you're planning some late night reading, Lauterbach? I hope you intend to share those 'books' with the other officers."

Lauterbach looked confused for a moment, then, understanding, pointed at the booze as if asking: "Do you mean these, sir?" He laughed a belly laugh, saluted a second time, and then straightened up, adopting the pose of some famous orator. He thrust his hand in the air and bellowed in English: "Send not to know for whom the bell tolls, it ..."

But Müller, who was also an accomplished English speaker, cut him off: "It will toll for thee if you don't assemble your booty in the ward room in forty-five minutes." The captain boarded, shaking his head, rolling his eyes, and mumbling half-disapprovingly, half-admiringly: "Lauterbach!"

•   •   •

On August 13th at the appointed hour Graf Spee welcomed the squadron captains into his suite. He stood on one side of the long conference table where he had spoken with Müller the day before, flanked by his chief of staff, Captain Fielitz, and the staff chief's second, Captain Pfahl. Filing into the room and along the other side of the table were Captain Schultz of *Scharnhorst*, Captain Maerker of *Gneisenau*, Captain Schönberg of *Nürnberg*, Captain Thiereken of *Prince Eitel Friedrich*, and *Emden*'s skipper, who flashed a look of concern at Spee: "He looks like he hasn't slept a wink," thought Müller. The admiral greeted each captain by name and ship. He nodded to each and each one saluted his admiral.

The salutation between Spee and Maerker, his close and longtime friend, bridge partner, and fellow natural history enthusiast, was especially warm. Unlike the others, *Gneisenau*'s captain had brought along his first officer, Lieutenant Commander Hans Pochhammer, like Müller an advocate of *guerre de course*, and someone Maerker considered his indispensable right-hand man, having been on the China station, and aboard the *Gneisenau*, much longer than his captain. Spee greeted him too. Then he asked all to be seated.

Remaining standing, Spee walked over to the wall map. A long wooden pointer lay at the base of the map. He picked it up and began to speak.

"As we all know, Japan will soon declare war on Germany—this is a probability bordering on certainty—which means it's impossible for us to remain in the Western Pacific. I prefer not to disperse the squadron—united we are a force that will draw a great number of enemy ships into the hunt. Our magazines are full, but we will be cut off from the ammunition depot in Tsingtao, our only means of resupply."

"Coal presents another problem. The heavy cruisers must refuel every eight or nine days and we are also cut off from our good Chinese coal."

"So I propose to sail for Chile, replenishing our fuel in Germany's Marshall Islands, augmenting our strength with *Leipzig*. Chile is friendly and our agents will have stored enough coal there to refill every ship and collier in the squadron. If we round the Horn our agents in Argentina and New York will have additional ample stores waiting for us."

"Our mission," he concluded, keeping his real operational intentions to himself in this more open forum, "will be to wage vigorous commerce warfare against the English."

"I've thought about this for days, and most of last night. What is your view of the situation, gentlemen?"

Schultz stood up and moved to the map, accepting the pointer from Spee. "I agree to the move east across the Pacific to guarantee a supply of coal, but why don't we raid an enemy port before departing? Here, at Vladivostok, or here, at Hong Kong. We could surprise and overpower warships and throw enemy commerce into a panic."

Still standing, and out of Schultz's way, Spee disagreed. "Raiding a port and sowing panic is a capital idea," said the admiral, although the look on his face signaled that he thought it less than capital. "But we'll shoot up too many shells needed later. Worse, in the three or four days it takes us to do it Japan could declare war, block our path east, and probably destroy the squadron. Are there other views?"

One by one, in order down the table moving away from the map, Maerker, Schönberg, and Thiereken said that they agreed with Spee. The latter two said this somewhat submissively after Maerker, who had known Spee long enough to be frank, had seemed somewhat skeptical.

As Müller's turn came he approached the map and received the pointer. As he handed it over, Spee frowned, as if thinking he would not like what he was about to hear.

"Gentlemen," he paused, "*comrades*, you know my theories," said Müller, acknowledging with the thrust of his chin that he was confident about convincing them. "Admiral Spee, with all due respect, I don't think keeping the squadron together is the best way to inflict harm on the enemy. As we steam east, taking months to reach the coast of Chile, we will neither do harm to his commerce, because we will be out of the regular shipping lanes, nor to enemy warships, for he won't commit ships to a chase across the Pacific, rather he will probably simply wait for us with a flotilla of a few battle cruisers—big fast ships built with the sole purpose of sinking ships like ours—here, in the Caribbean, in case he thinks we choose to pass through the new Panama Canal, and another here, in the Falkland Islands, if he thinks we will round Cape Horn. Unless battleships from the home fleet reinforce us, we're badly outgunned."

"I propose, gentlemen, that we move west—not east, but west—into the Indian Ocean to reinforce the lone ship we have there, light cruiser *Königsberg*, based in East Africa . To force the enemy to commit the largest number of ships against us we should break the squadron up to raid commerce. The heavy cruisers will take two colliers apiece, both light cruisers and *Prinz Eitel Friedrich* one each. We will not only throw commerce into a panic, but damage British prestige to the point of triggering an Indian Mutiny that will make that of 1857 look like child's play. Capturing coal from their merchant ships at sea, and using the Dutch East Indies as a haven, we can operate indefinitely."

He paused for a long moment. "However, as an alternative, if coaling will be a bigger problem than I anticipate, we should consider sending at least one cruiser west."

After this appeal, he took his seat. Spee too. Around the table the captains were nodding approval and casting positive glances at one another—surface raiding might indeed be a good idea. Fielitz was nodding too and spoke first. "Admiral, all or part of this could work. I believe that we should send *at least* one cruiser west."

Pochhammer, the most junior man in rank present, had kept silent thus far, but now joined Fielitz: "Respectfully, Admiral Spee, it seems to me that we can best hurt Britain by threatening her base of power—her empire.

She will rush to protect it, and in so doing abandon her allies in Europe to their fate."

Sensing the consensus moving away from what he wanted, Spee, still keeping his composure but looking even more fatigued, took back control. "I, too, have considered taking the whole squadron west. But we have no coaling bases in the Indian Ocean and no agents whom we can get in touch with. The Dutch will never allow us haven or provide us with enough coal lest they bend the laws of neutrality too far and give the Japanese the excuse they are looking for to declare war on Holland and seize the East Indies. All that we will accomplish, without the strength of the united squadron, is to be hunted down one by one. I needn't remind you that Australia fights for Britain, and they have a new battle cruiser, HMAS *Australia*."

"Gentlemen, thank you for your opinions. Return to your ships and raise steam. I'll make my final decision and issue orders within the hour."

· · ·

Forty-five minutes later *Scharnhorst*'s launch delivered orders to the squadron. On board *Gneisenau* Pochhammer found Captain Maerker on the bridge and read out Spee's decision: "At 1730 hours weigh anchor and set a course east-southeast for Eniwetok."

Maerker smiled and nodded, signaling his lack of surprise. "Well, Pochhammer, I hope the Japanese haven't set their course for east-southeast too."

Pochhammer looked alarmed. "I'd say the odds are better than even that that's exactly what they do, sir.

Legal formalities like *declaring war first* didn't stop them from sinking the Russian fleet at Port Arthur in 1905."

"You're quite right, Pochhammer," said Maerker, his expression showing the skepticism he felt for Graf Spee's decision.

Mücke also found his captain on the bridge, but the orders he read out were different: "Accompanied by the steamship *Markomannia*, you are to be detached for deployment into the eastern Indian Ocean, there to wage a vigorous war against enemy commerce to the best of your ability. Good luck to you and to SMS *Königsberg*."

As the small fleet left Pagan the warships formed a line to port, *Prince Eitel Friedrich* and the colliers to starboard. They steamed through the night. At 0800 on August 14th *Scharnhorst* signaled *Emden*: "*Emden* detached."

Emden signaled *Markomannia*, and a few minutes later they both reversed course and headed southwest. As they turned, *Emden* signaled *Scharnhorst*: "My dutiful thanks for the confidence placed in me. Success to the squadron and *Gute Reise*."

• • •

Germany's daring, noble corsair, Captain of the Imperial German Navy Karl von Müller, had signaled *Bon Voyage* to his admiral, Graf Maximilian von Spee. Two of the greatest adventures in the history of World War One had begun.

The fortunes of war, as Müller had said to Grant, are never always positive, but the East Asiatic Squadron would now attempt to rain down terrible destruction, horrific death, and anguishing defeat on enemy heads. Although Müller and Spee succeeded in becoming legends in their time, neither would escape the ghosts of enemy dead, and of dead comrades too, who called them to account from watery graves. And how would they answer loved ones in Britain, France, Russia, and Germany who wanted only to see uncles, husbands, brothers, and sons again?

VI
THE DUTCH EAST INDIES

For five days we steamed southwest from the Marianas toward Anguar in the Palau Islands, the westernmost chain of the German Carolines. Many of the crew expressed surprise at first, for early rumors that *Emden* would engage in solo raiding seemed false when we left Pagan with the squadron. But astonishment quickly gave way to excitement and anxiety: any glory we achieved would be ours alone, we could become the stuff of sea legend. Or we could meet with a swift, violent, and bloody end. And we all worried about Graf Spee and the rest of the squadron. Had the enemy concentrated superior numbers against them? Could they make it home?

On some days the sun bore down cruelly, turning decks into boiler plates, a mirage of heat waves rising from all surfaces. At other times torrents of rain fell, every drop hissing and steaming as it hit. But we had work to do through all of this. My officers and I worried about the crew's state of readiness. Many of the men had only joined the ship weeks before the visit of the *Minotaur*. They were not fully drilled. So we had the gun crews train their barrels over and over again on *Markomannia*. When a real target appeared suddenly they had to be able to hit it quickly and accurately. This would be more serious business than a friendly target shoot against the English in the bay at Tsingtao. Winch crews repeatedly drilled in hoisting shells from the magazines below decks, while squads of shell carriers vied with one another to rapidly stack shell cases behind the 4.1-inch guns. Daily winners got cigars.

The gun crews had another important task to practice. To make a shell ready to explode, the metal fuse cylinder must be screwed into the nose of the shell—and, importantly, the cap screw on the end of the fuse screwed off and then screwed back in reverse position. Otherwise the shell's safety is in the "on" not the "off" position and the shell will not detonate. This has to be practiced until gun crews can do it automatically in the stress and terrifying steely rattle of battle. To fail here meant disaster for a warship.

Our four bow and stern guns had armor shields to protect against shell fragments and splinters, but Mücke and I worried about the six blister mounts amidships, so we fashioned woven hemp shields around the casemates.

Underway we wired our radio station on Yap, a few hundred miles from our position, but heard no response. This added to our anxiety because a collier had been dispatched there to augment *Markomannia*. Later we learned that this ship and the wireless station on Yap had been destroyed by the *Minotaur* and another older British armored cruiser, probably our future pursuer HMS *Hampshire*, on August 12th, the very day *Emden* reached Pagan Island. If London had let them prowl these waters we could very well have run into them. Badly outgunned, our ship and four hundred men would have been blown sky high. Against Admiral Jerram's better judgment, however, First Lord of the Admiralty Winston Churchill ordered the cruisers back to guard Hong Kong, which Graf Spee had decided not to attack. Happily for us we had in Mr. Churchill an involuntary ally.

Coaling in the harbor at Anguar was much more arduous than coaling at Tsingtao—and now we had no Chinese coolies to do it. The crew responded to the challenge with humor. They could not wear a regular uniform for this filthy work anyway, so instead they donned comical makeshift costumes: a fantastic outfit from a crossing of the equator initiation; a worn out dress suit and top hat without crown; and the like.[2] These comical fellows helped put everyone in a good mood, despite the hard work. To make the long hours of labor somewhat more tolerable, the ship's band always played rousing march music. Between songs the officers and I offered peppy words of encouragement. Comedy, entertainment, and speeches aside, however, rapid completion of this labor was absolutely essential for the safety of the ship because we were so vulnerable to surprise attack when coaling dead in the water. Even a smaller destroyer could have made short work of us with torpedoes, one of the deadliest weapons at sea.

---

2   From Pochhammer, *Before Jutland*. See my methodological After-word.

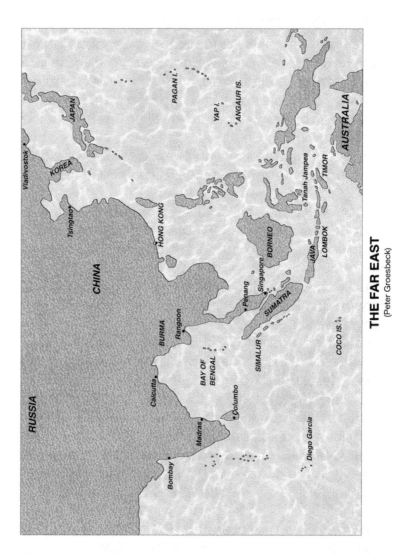

THE FAR EAST
(Peter Groesbeck)

Emden drew alongside *Markomannia*, put down fenders over the side, made fast to the collier, and laid down the gangways. Below in the bunkers of our collier sailors shoveled the good Chinese coal into double shoulder sacks that they hoisted up to the deck. Men topside slung the heavy sacks over their shoulders, walked carefully over the gangways, which pitched and rolled with the sea, and dumped their loads down chutes into *Emden*'s bunkers. Comrades below, wearing goggles and placing sponges in their mouths to combat the dust, shoveled the fuel so that the bunker filled up evenly. They filled the bunker so full that they had to creep out of it on all fours. It was backbreaking, filthy work, especially in the heat of the tropics with sweat turning the coal dust into black oily grime. Once finished in the bunkers we loaded extra life-saving coal into huge mounds on deck.

After coaling in the Palaus, *Emden* resumed her southwesterly course, steaming through the Straits of Mollucca, and then due south to the Portuguese island of Timor, where we coaled again on August 25th. Once again a rendezvous with a collier was missed when no German steamship was there to meet us. While taking on coal we learned that Japan had declared war against us two days earlier.

We proceeded into the Dutch East Indies on the 26th, passing many small volcanic islands, beautiful Timor to port, its tropical heights, so full of vegetation, rising to eight thousand feet. We enjoyed the momentary luxury of nature's work of art, but war's ever-present perils tempered our enjoyment. Was it any different inside the beautiful thick rain forest we viewed? Indeed, the only law observed there was that of the jungle. Soon enough we left Timor behind and steamed ahead to Tanah Jampea Island, where Admiralty had sent yet another collier, the *Offenbach*, to join us.

. . .

On the morning of August 27th the German cruiser approached Tanah Jampea from the south, skirted the eastern side of the island, and turned hard to port to enter its northern bay. The speaking tube on the bridge had a message. Müller listened, and then turned to Mücke: "The radio room is picking up a heavy flow of signals from a warship—probably Dutch."

Suddenly across a spit of land the two saw the warship racing along the northern side of the island at full steam, 3,000 meters to starboard. They both hurried to the right side, onto the flying (or captain's) bridge, and raised their binoculars. "She's flying battle ensigns, but what nationality?!" said the first officer alarmingly.

"No time to wait and see," came the curt reply. "Sound battle stations, hoist the top flags," the captain ordered sternly.

As the crew scrambled to their battle stations, drums rolling and alarm bells sounding, set fuses, loaded shells, and trained the five starboard guns on the bow of the approaching ship, tension thickened. Would this be *Emden*'s first action? The other vessel was bigger—could it be Jerram's light cruiser *Yarmouth* with her 6-inch guns? Or worse, maybe the 9.2-inch guns of *Minotaur* herself? While every gun crew tensed for the order to fire, and shell carriers brought extra ordnance, the captain and first officer strained through their binoculars at the ship's ensigns to identify them. Suddenly Müller said with some relief: "She's Dutch, lower the top flags."

The intruder was a Dutch coastal defense battleship, the *Tromp*, somewhat antiquated but carrying 8-inch guns. She lowered her ensigns, turned to starboard, and led *Emden* into the bay. As both ships dropped anchor, Müller's crew still eyed the Dutchman warily.

According to sea custom the captain of a smaller ship paid the first visit, so after a pause to clean *Emden*'s launch and don dress whites, the small party set off for the *Tromp*, where Müller was greeted by Captain Umbgrove and shown to the wardroom for a glass of beer. After pleasantries and small talk, Umbgrove turned to business as Müller listened politely.

"As you know, captain, Holland is neutral in this war. I have orders to observe the laws of neutrality strictly— *to make no exceptions*—lest Japan seize on any pretext to take over our colonies in the Far East, which they have long coveted. Accordingly, I ordered your collier to put to sea again two days ago. She had exceeded the 24-hour limit allowed under international law in neutral waters. My government's policy on warships is, I'm afraid, the strict interpretation of the law. Men-of-war are allowed only one 24-hour coaling and provisioning stop in our waters *every three months*."

As Umbgrove finished, Müller leaned forward in his chair with a look of surprise, then settled back, thinking for a brief moment: "So, Graf Spee was right. Surface raiding will be much tougher than I thought." Then, trying to ameliorate an already awkward situation, he finally replied to the Dutch captain. "But, of course, captain, the German Empire respects the rights of neutral nations. *Emden* will resume her voyage immediately."

Müller had unwittingly added to the awkwardness. Umbgrove's eyebrows raised at the mention of rights of neutrality, a smile of incredulity coming over his face as he thought: "Yes, look at the respect Germany showed neutral Belgium, which is now conquered and occupied by German hordes—will Holland be next?!" Then Umbgrove remembered his duties as host. "But before you go, captain, may I entertain you and your officers with a few rounds of drinks?"

Müller politely declined the offer, returned to the *Emden*, weighed anchor, and put to sea, accompanied to the three-mile limit by the *Tromp*.

•   •   •

Mücke and I discussed what all of this meant and determined that the situation was less grave than we first thought. Lauterbach knew of many isolated island coves in Java and Sumatra where we could provision the ship with food and water and take on coal from our collier without the Dutch knowing about it. What they—and the Japanese—didn't know would not hurt them.

But if our luck was to hold we had to be cleverer than the enemy, and after the lucky avoidance of *Minotaur* and *Hampshire* or *Newcastle* then the brief scare with *Tromp*, Mücke came up with a brilliant idea, a stroke of genius. We fashioned a fourth funnel made out of canvas and reinforced with wooden ribs. It could be hoisted on a moment's notice and secured to our rear mast, thus disguising our ship by giving it the distinctive appearance of a British four-funneled cruiser or destroyer. As we steamed west toward the straits between Lombock and Bali—the passageway into the Indian Ocean—the radio room received reports of a four-funneled ship in the vicinity, so we had to work fast. The phantom funnel was hoisted at dusk on August 28th as *Emden* approached the straits. After a fortunately uneventful night, dawn found us through the narrows and into the Indian Ocean.

For the next six days *Emden* steamed west off the southern coast of Java, then northwesterly along the entire length of Sumatra. Lauterbach knew an out-of-the-way cove on the northeastern end of Simalur, just a few days steaming south of the Bay of Bengal and its busy shipping lanes, where I hoped to begin taking prizes.

Cruising at only twelve knots to minimize fuel consumption *Emden* did not need to use all of her twelve boilers, which afforded us a good opportunity to accelerate the normal work of boiler maintenance on those that were not generating steam. For a boiler to work properly its inside walls must be scrubbed every five days, and more thoroughly every twenty days. Every ten days its water has to be changed and all corrosive materials cleaned from the zinc panels. And just as regularly we had to clean all fourteen hundred pipes in a boiler by tediously pulling a wire brush through each one of them. During our voyage we also replaced hundreds of faulty pipes. Finally, the condensers that desalinated ocean water for all kinds of uses on board had to be frequently scrubbed clean of salt.

All of these tasks, which we called "working in the mines," were just as essential to the success of our mission as the speed, precision, and accuracy of the gun crews or the time it took the crew to complete coaling. When the moment of battle came, *Emden* had to have all twelve boilers working properly to ensure maximum speed—and maximum chance of outmaneuvering the enemy.

As *Emden* approached Simalur, I reduced speed in order to arrive in the cove on the morning of September 4th. All day on the 2nd and 3rd the radio operator had reported to the bridge the presence of a warship using the identifying call sign "QMD." *Emden* had last heard this signal on August 12th, the day *Minotaur* and probably *Hampshire* bombarded Yap. After much debate the officers had decided—correctly as it turned out—that the call sign was *Hampshire*'s, so we had to be careful.

We learned later that Grant's ship had indeed been in the area, searching the cove on September 3rd, and then anchoring off the southern tip of Simalur that night, steaming away in a southerly direction next morning. On our way in the darkness on the 3rd, and totally blacked out, we passed only twenty miles from her anchorage. Once again our luck had held.

During our coaling another Dutch coastal defense vessel spotted us. We once again heard a lecture on Holland's strict interpretation of the laws of neutrality. Now I had to abandon all thought of secretly using Dutch waters as a haven. My admiral, it appeared, had been far wiser than I. Admitting this lifted my spirits a bit, however, because if Graf Spee had guessed right about the Dutch, maybe his instincts would guide the rest of the squadron successfully back to the Fatherland.

At 1100 hours on September 5th, our coaling completed, we headed for the shipping lanes, all of us anxious for our first action *and our first prize* in these waters.

VII
THE BAY OF BENGAL

On September 7th Müller's raider reached the shipping routes leading from Ceylon and southern India to Sumatra. He raised the phantom funnel to lull prey into thinking they were a British ship on patrol. But the spirits of officers and crew sagged as two days passed without the lookouts spying so much as a single funnel or smoke trail. Depressingly empty of commerce, the sea seemed to mock them.

After the disappointments of Tanah Jampea and Simalur, the captain who so wanted to prove his worth to his family, his admiral, and his emperor disappeared into the chart room behind the bridge for hours on end, catching only an occasional cat nap in one of the chairs he had commandeered from Lauterbach. His mood sour, the man in charge snapped at the crew. On September 9th he abandoned these waters and headed for the shipping lane between Ceylon and Burma.

At 2300 the lookout in the foremast yelled down: "Lights four points to starboard!" No warship hunting for *Emden* would be so lit up at night—it must be a merchantman.

Müller was awakened and notified. Seconds later, he commanded the officer of the watch: "All ahead full. Clear the ship for action." Then, turning to Mücke: "Get Lauterbach to assemble a boarding party."

After the distance to the steamer narrowed to a hundred meters, a Morse lamp spelled out in English: "Stop your engines. Do not use the wireless." The ship obeyed immediately. Lauterbach and his hand-picked team rowed in the ship's cutter to the prize. They hurried up the Jacob's ladder, followed by their leader, all armed to the teeth, the whole scene illuminated by *Emden*'s huge masthead search lights. Müller and Mücke waited anxiously on the bridge for Lauterbach to signal the ship's identity and cargo.

Finally he flashed: "Greek steamship, *Pontoporos*." The captain and his first officer cast disappointed glances at one another. Müller swore: "Damn it! She's neutral and we can't touch her!" Destiny seemed against the corsairs: Greece had proclaimed neutrality, so *Emden* could not claim this ship as a prize.

"What about the cargo, Lauterbach," said Mücke angrily, and then added even more emphatically: "Is her cargo also neutral!?"

But just then Lauterbach finished his message. "Carrying 6,500 tons of coal for English government. Is on her way from Calcutta to Bombay."

An English contraband cargo was prize worthy—and *Pontoporos* carried more coal than *Markomannia* fully loaded. "Signal Lauterbach to seize the ship and follow us to starboard," ordered Müller, a very confident look having wiped away the previously worried countenance. "How many more like this one around?"

he said, still looking, somewhat arrogantly, as he thought to himself that fate had probably vindicated him: "I was right after all. My Indian Ocean strategy for the squadron would have worked."

During the night *Emden* and her two sisters entered the shipping lane between Colombo and Calcutta off the east coast of India. At 0700 on the following day Müller sent another officer over to *Pontoporos* to replace Lauterbach. The indispensable big fellow might soon be needed again.

And, sure enough, at 0900 lookouts spotted a smoke trail on the horizon. Müller barked orders for full speed and clearing for action, hundreds of feet thumping the decks on their urgent way to battle stations. The steamer steered unsuspectingly toward the four-funneled warship. Suddenly *Emden* ran up her German battle ensigns and fired a shot from the forward starboard gun across the ship's bow. She too was ordered to stop engines and send no wireless messages.

Lauterbach picked another band of pirates and rowed to the new prize of war. His ten-man party went up the Jacobs ladder and fanned out, two by two, to their guard positions. When Lauterbach's turn at the ladder came he slipped off the second rung and fell backwards into the water, making a splash worthy of his great bulk. Looking appropriately embarrassed, he hoisted himself arm over arm high enough to secure a rung with one foot, then much more competently ascended. Never lacking stage presence, he turned around to face the *Emden* and bowed triumphantly, sharing with the entire observing German crew a good laugh at himself.

Lauterbach entered the captain's cabin with two of his men to stand guard inside the door. "Ship's manifest if you please," he said politely to the British skipper.

"What do you think you are doing boarding my ship with armed men?" replied the indignant captain.

"Merely observing international law," said Lauterbach sarcastically. "I can't help it if your empire declared war on mine. Your ship is under German martial law," he said, pointing to his men. "Now if you don't mind, the manifest please."

After it was reluctantly produced, Lauterbach sat down to inspect it, then after just a few seconds looked up at his host: "In our navy it's customary to offer drinks when sailors of other nations come calling." The Brit, looking dumbfounded, was speechless. Lauterbach pointed to the liquor cabinet as if to say "over there, that's what I mean."

A bottle and glasses were procured. The British captain, the meaning of his circumstances beginning to sink in, downed his shot quickly. Lauterbach, feigning offense at not being allowed to drink the round together, raised his glass, took a sip, swirled it around his mouth mocking an expert wine taster, swallowed, and said "cheers."

This prize, the *Indus*, carried provisions for a regiment of the Indian army it had orders to pick up in Bombay and take to Europe. Soon *Emden*'s cutters and its launch began removing the cargo: chickens and livestock and enough canned goods, potatoes, cheese, chocolates, soap, and water for 3,000 men.

The *Indus* also regurgitated a great quantity of booze and cigarettes for the regiment's British officers and NCOs. Mücke distributed the booty among the various divisions of the crew: the officers, the gunners, the magazine crews and shell carriers, the torpedo crew, the radiomen, the stokers, and so on, all receiving their fair share. The German corsairs got ready to live the life of pirate royalty.

With the looting completed, the crew removed to *Markomannia*, explosive charges laid, the sea cocks opened, and the charges detonated, the ship began slowly to sink. *Emden*'s crew watched in silence, for the end of a vessel—any vessel—was no cause for rejoicing by men of the sea who knew all too well that a similar fate could befall them too. As the ocean claimed more and more of its victim, one of the stokers bellowed: "Look there mates, she beckons. *Indus* awaits us below."

Because the sinking took too long for an impatient Müller, he ordered shots fired at the waterline. As three shells burst into the doomed vessel one after the other in rapid succession, the sight was too much for the British captain. Standing with Lauterbach at the railing outside the wardroom, he broke down. Lauterbach at first looked as if he thought this unmanly, then, turning more sympathetic, escorted the unfortunate man into the wardroom and served up another round of drinks. He said kindly: "Fortunes of war, captain, fortunes of war."

· · ·

Over the next five days Müller captured and sank four more vessels. He also seized a fifth, the *Kabinga*, but then released her with the crews of *Emden*'s first six victims aboard. All had been treated well according to international law. Even though he had brooked no rebelliousness from this growing throng of hundreds of enemy sailors, posting notices in three languages on the collier that resistance to German authority would be punishable by death, the captain still managed to acquire a reputation for fairness and restraint. As *Kabinga* headed away toward the shores of India, the former captives lined the deck and offered up three cheers to their captors.

Müller acknowledged the salute, but his thoughts continued to dwell on the calculus of recent success: indeed, if he could sustain the current frenetic pace of taking prizes the confident prediction to Graf Spee of "one hundred or more" ships taken by the entire squadron would be achieved by *Emden* alone in four or five months.

On September 16th Müller sensed he had been too long in the same waters, so he headed northeast across the Bay of Bengal toward Rangoon. Because the sea that day was sufficiently moderate to permit coaling—and this had again become necessary—he decided to do this. Coaling on the open sea, however, was going to be much more of a challenge than in a sheltered cove, not to mention Tsingtao. And with the ship vulnerable to attack the task had to be done quickly.

Emden and *Pontoporos* pitched and rolled with the heavy swells, prey upon the vast watery prairie of the Indian Ocean. Lookouts scanned the horizons from masthead perches, exposed little creatures nervously glancing around for predators that might swoop in at any second to disrupt the risky, grimy work. A storm cloud fifteen miles to port? Or a smoke trail?

The crew used makeshift tenders made of tree trunks and automobile tires to replace the originals, which had long since been bashed into a useless condition. The sailors on *Pontoporos* waited for both ships to roll together. At this moment the weighty coal sacks suspended from ropes and pulleys were swung over to *Emden*, then the ropes released, such that the sacks crashed anywhere and everywhere on the warship, sailors franticly dodging the fuel bags lest they be the ship's first casualties. Railings, davits, and funnels became dented.

A normally imperturbable Müller presided anxiously over all of this from the flying bridge. "Keep a sharp eye out sailor," he yelled up to a watcher in the foremast. His attention switched back to the assault of the violent coal sacks. He looked nervously at his wrist watch. Just then one sack slammed into the forward gun blister below him, wrecking the hemp screen and hitting the gun barrel. Müller, his anxiety continuing to mount, barked angrily at the crewman whose aim had been so poor: "You hit my gun again and I'll have you keel-hauled!"

The mortified sailor snapped to attention and cried: "Aye, aye captain! It won't happen again!"

The captain cast a glance at his dented, dirty ship. "Our white swan has become a black swan," he thought, "and we know what happens to black swans. Bad omen, bad omen."

• • •

The coaling finished, the small flotilla continued on its northeasterly heading. On September 17th and all day of the 18th they cruised the eastern Bay of Bengal, but spotted only one ship from neutral Norway, which could not be taken.

During the night Guérard yelled into the speaking tube to the bridge that he had picked up the call sign 'QMD' again. The signal was strong, so *Hampshire* could not be far away. The next night the signal was even stronger—the hunter had to be within ten miles. Müller reversed course and steamed back across the Bay toward India. The signals were no longer heard.

He had another plan of action: to bombard the tanks of the Burma Oil Company in Madras and destroy any tankers or warships in the harbor. Captain Grant had guessed correctly that Madras would be *Emden*'s next target and therefore steamed west to destroy her—hence the call signs that grew daily stronger. *Hampshire* had to turn back, however, to investigate what turned out to be a false report of a German threat to Burma. A big Japanese battle cruiser in the Indian Ocean, the *Ibuki*, had also been ordered to rendezvous at Madras, but lost its chance to destroy the raider by taking two entire days to coal in Colombo. Fate continued to smile on SMS *Emden*.

VIII
MADRAS AND CEYLON

At 0900 on September 21st, while continuing to pursue his westerly heading toward the targeted city, Müller convened a wardroom council of the top-ranking officers who were in charge of the various divisions of the ship.

"Gentlemen, tomorrow evening I intend to shell the oil-tank installations of Madras. The secondary object of our mission is to do damage to British commerce, but the primary objective is to further diminish British prestige. From the newspapers brought on board from our prize ships we know that British authorities have sought to belittle our successes, hoping thereby to avoid panic in business circles, and to avoid rebelliousness among the Indian people. 'We will soon be sunk,' they boast—one report already has us at the bottom of the ocean."

"Gentlemen, tomorrow we will put the lie to these accounts and demonstrate to all India that mighty Britain is not so mighty, that one lone ship can roam the sea at will, and lash out with impunity. If the Indian population is as rife with seditiousness as all of our pre-war reports indicated, the rebels in India may be emboldened to rise up. They must know, as we do, that troop ship after troop ship is carrying the Indian Army to other theaters of action. With no mongoose in the yard, a snake will strike."

"Mücke, carry on from here." He rose, and as he did the others rose too, then he turned and left the room.

"Gentlemen, be seated," said the first officer. "The harbor has old 6.3 inch guns, but big enough to do us considerable damage. If a lucky shot or two kills the captain, and me, each of you must be prepared to complete the mission, hence this briefing."

Spreading a map of the harbor before him, Mücke continued. "We will enter the harbor obliquely from the northeast with the oil tanks dead ahead to the southwest. With the town itself off to starboard, any salvo that overshoots the target will not fall into residential areas. We will defeat our primary purpose if we kill civilians and convince the Indian people that we Germans are bigger monsters than the English."

"At 3,000 meters from shore we will turn to port, spotlight the tanks, and fire repeated salvos from our starboard batteries. Once the installation is destroyed, and any shipping in the harbor also destroyed, we will steam back to the northeast, illuminated, as a ruse. Once out of sight of shore we will black out, reverse course, and head south. Any questions?"

The torpedo room officer of the *Emden* was none other than the Kaiser's nephew, Prince Franz Josef von Hohenzollern, who had a question. Not wishing to treat him any differently than the other officers, Mücke said simply: "Yes Hohenzollern." The young prince asked if torpedoes would be required in the attack. "Probably not," said Mücke, "unless we encounter a warship in the harbor, so stand ready. Anything else?"

As there were no further questions at this point, he continued. "All right, gentlemen, here are your orders for today and tomorrow. He spoke, in turn, to each officer responsible for the functions he mentioned: "Targeting drills for the gunners and torpedo crew. Magazine crews and shell carriers: double the supply of ordnance at each gun. Stow the canvas shade awnings below decks—they are a fire hazard. Fill the lifeboats with water to minimize fire damage. Ship's crew will bathe and be issued clean uniforms to prevent infection from wounds. Engine room, ready ten boilers for fire at top speed by 2000 hours tomorrow. *Markomannia*, you will be detached at 1800 tomorrow. Rendezvous with *Emden* next day off Pondicherry. That's it, gentlemen, hop to."

• • •

At 2000 hours on September 22nd the captain left the chart room, descended the stairs to the armored conning tower below, and gave his orders: "Battle stations. Hoist the top flags. All ahead full."

Emden cut through the water toward Madras, blacked out, an assassin shrouded in darkness. Every man stood at his station, tensed for the ship's first battle. At 2140, with the ship 3,000 meters from shore, Müller ordered: "Hard to port. Stop engines."

A few minutes passed, then he barked: "Search lights on, fire when ready, Gaede!"

Seconds later the gunnery officer on the bridge, Lieutenant Commander Gaede, sent his order electronically to the five starboard rifle mounts: "Open fire!" The guns belched fire and smoke in awesome, well-drilled unison. Their deafening thunderbolt claps destroyed the silence of a calm late summer night.

Mücke, the lookout in the fore mast, yelled down that the first salvo had overshot the tanks by a hundred meters. Quickly, Gaede transmitted orders electrically to the officers of the gun crews to lower the barrels a few degrees of elevation, and then a moment later, seeing that the guns had been re-aimed, again pushed his button: "Fire!" The second salvo smashed into the first tank and set it ablaze.

Prince Franz Joseph and his good friend, Lieutenant Ernst von Levetzow, watched the action from port side aft. Levetzow, himself quite distinguished as scion of a famous German military family, had been assigned by the admiralty to accompany the young prince aboard the *Emden*. As commander of the aft port gun, he was not involved in this action. Lauterbach, also not required for this operation, stood alongside the two friends. When the first tank exploded, all three roared their cheers, which mixed with those of the rest of the crew. "*Deutschland hoch, der Kaiser hoch!*" they all screamed.

In ten minutes, 125 shots careened violently down on the installation, lighting up the sky south of Madras. Two of the six tanks burned, while three others that had been empty were badly damaged. The fort managed to get off a few shots at the intruder, which missed badly, but the captain quickly ordered the search lights turned off lest the aim from shore improve.

At 2150 Müller ordered: "Start engines, hard to port, full speed ahead." *Emden* stole away from view into the darkened ocean, having delivered her message explosively to Britain—and to India— in cold hard steel and cordite-yellowed smoke. Then, just as planned, the corsair turned about once land was out of sight.

• • •

Our mission achieved its secondary objective. The oily inferno remained visible from the bridge throughout the night despite the great distance we rapidly put between us and Madras. The next morning, eighty miles out to sea, we could still see the smoking tanks on the horizon. All of this gave visual testimony to our victory.

From newspapers that fell into our hands we learned that our primary objective had met with considerable success too. All along the east coast of India, from Pondicherry to Calcutta, people fled, fearing that their towns would be victims of the next raid. British authorities tried to downplay the danger and again predicted our impending destruction, but their efforts backfired. One news report from Calcutta put it this way: "*The British are embittered, and with good reason, because all of the Indians they are in contact with have overblown ideas about Germany's might. The assurances of the sahibs that Great Britain and her allies are heading toward victory are not believed by the native population.*"

Soon after our raid a wave of violence swept the northern province of Punjab. "*There has been a constant series of explosions*," ran another report. "*All over the Punjab police have been murdered and loyal citizens, especially those known to be assisting the authorities, have been shot down or killed by bombs*." We also read about native soldiers deserting the Indian Army in large numbers.

Yes, it seemed that Britain's days in India were numbered, that a huge blow had been struck against the might of the British Empire—and to the British war effort. But as the weeks passed we looked in vain for reports of the great uprising, the second great Indian Mutiny we thought we had incited. Alas, the British had plenty of guns and the people only a few. A handful of scattered bomb-making factories in hidden cellars and attics amounted to little, moreover, against the remaining divisions of Britain's Indian Army. If only we had been able to capture a ship loaded with weapons and ammunition, and then get these into the right hands, it might have been different.

Later, as prisoners aboard the *Hampshire*, Captain Grant told us that the German government had indeed been plotting to do just this. A ship, the *Bayern*, crammed to the gunnels with 500,000 pistols, 100,000 rifles, and 200,000 cases of ammunition had orders for the Far East in August 1914, but the Italians interned this veritable floating arsenal a day after the war broke out. The fortunes of war would have frowned on British India if the *Bayern* had been only a few days farther along on her journey, through the Suez Canal and steaming into the Indian Ocean, but this was not to be. British rule in India survived the war, if only by a hair.

From the newspapers and a few of our captives we learned that the English were not just concerned with our ship, but also with the *Königsberg*, which was taking prizes and sowing panic off the Red Sea and East Africa—*Nürnberg*'s sister ship had even raided the harbor at Zanzibar and sunk a Royal Navy cruiser and gunboat. After reading about the Zanzibar raid I longed for a chance to test *our* mettle against English men-of-war.

For the moment, however, the men of the *Emden* went in search of more prizes. We were resolved to further embarrass Britannia and embolden Indian rebels, but wondering all the while what might have been if our entire East Asiatic Squadron had steamed west, not east. What if a full squadron of cruisers hunted in Britain's lake with us? What if *Scharnhorst* and *Gneisenau* had bombarded Calcutta, administrative capital of British India, while we hit Madras, *Nürnberg* shelled Colombo, *Leipzig* attacked Bombay, and *Königsberg* raided Mombasa, having already struck at Zanzibar? Would not panicky alarm bells have gone off heard all the way in London? How much of the Royal Navy would Churchill have sent racing to the heart of his empire?

Steering around Ceylon on September 25th and into the rich shipping lane between Colombo and the Red Sea, we took prizes in rapid succession, six more ships in only four days, four of which we sunk, while one, the *Buresk*, loaded with 6,600 tons of the best Welsh coal, we attached to our little flotilla. We released another prize ship with all of the captured crews and ordered it to take the captives to the safety of the nearest British port. Our reputation as gentlemen warriors, men of honor, was growing.

Fearing that our pursuers would close the ring on us if we stayed any longer in these waters, I headed south on September 30th, far out of the regular shipping lanes, to the Chagos Archipelago, there to rest the crew, take on coal and provisions, and perform long overdue maintenance on the ship. It was especially important to cant the *Emden*, scrape off the barnacles that had reduced our top speed by a few knots, and then repaint the hull.

After many days at sea we steamed into the bay of Diego Garcia. Although this was a British island, Lauterbach knew that there was no naval base there, no European settlement, in fact only two Europeans, an Englishman and a French speaker from Madagascar, neither of whom, as it turned out, had received any news from the outside world for three months—they did not even know that Britain and France were now at war with Germany. So we plied them with drinks and amused ourselves by telling them ridiculous stories about what we were doing in the area: that we were on maneuvers, and that the ship looked so beat up because we had just come through a storm.

The lack of news frustrated the officers and crew, however, for it prevented us from resolving what by this time had become a daily topic of hot debate and raging speculation. One big question still weighed on all of our minds:

Where was Graf Spee? We had read earlier in the newspapers about his ships appearing in Samoa and Tahiti—what was he doing there?! This news, however, was ten days old. Where was the East Asiatic now? Already sunk? Nearing Chile? Could they make it home?

IX
EAST TO ENIWETOK

On the afternoon of August 14th Hans Pochhammer had the watch on the bridge of SMS *Gneisenau*. It was one of those oven-hot equatorial days that made bodies ooze sweat even when sitting down motionless and trying to relax. The big ship's first officer paced back and forth from one side of the cruiser to the other, peering for a few moments out to sea through binoculars and then, dripping wet in his summer whites, repeating the drill on the other side.

Pochhammer had difficulty concentrating on his naval duties. His thoughts kept bouncing from the task at hand—spotting pursuing enemy warships—to what was happening oceans away. Back in Europe, had Germany won the first battles? Or, horrible to contemplate, had the jealous enemies of the Fatherland beaten back the German army? Had French and Russian soldiers crossed the border, raping, murdering, and pillaging? On this uncomfortably scorching summer day were his wife and two young sons still alive and safe?

• • •

After detaching *Emden*, Graf Spee took our ships on an east-southeasterly course for the German island of Eniwetok. That was four years ago, yet how very well I remember this day. Three warships, one auxiliary cruiser, and seven colliers, the core of the East Asiatic Squadron, steamed smartly in two columns away from Pagan Island, beaming resplendently in the hot Pacific sun, belching smoke from a small forest of funnels.

Hans Pochhammer: We were hunted
(Pochhammer, *Graf Spee's letzte Fahrt*)

But the impressive appearance of our squadron belied the mood of apprehension that gripped all of the officers and men. With thoughts of home tugging at our hearts, it was almost impossible to do our duty. But we had to—for we were the hunted, the enemy's quarry if caught. Lookouts in both masts of *Gneisenau* searched the horizons in all directions for our pursuers. We knew that Admiral Jerram had bombarded Yap two days earlier—if he guessed Spee's course to Eniwetok correctly, smoke trails from the southwest meant facing broadsides from four 9.2-inch and five 7.5-inch guns on *Minotaur*. She would never be strong enough to contend with the combined salvos of our armored cruisers, twelve 8.2-inch guns, but if we spotted an imposing tripod mast among the British ships, it meant that Jerram also sailed with a battle cruiser, HMAS *Australia*, whose 26 knots and broadsides from six 12-inch guns gave him a lopsided advantage.

Worse still, we knew that Japan had given the governor of Tsingtao an ultimatum: surrender the colony or prepare to defend it in war. Had the Japanese, assuming the obvious—that Germany would reject these insulting demands—already joined the hunt? Lookouts strained through their binoculars to see any sign to the north and west of Japan's modern navy, steaming into action at full speed with its dreadnought battleships, battle cruisers, and cruisers both heavy and light, fast and powerful ships that could sink the East Asiatic before our batteries could inflict harm. Dreadnought battleships and battle cruisers could open fire at 18,000 yards, while we needed to be closer to 12,000.

On August 15th the worry and apprehension that reigned among us heightened as a new threat blew up from the South Pacific.[3] Gale force winds slammed into our small fleet, wrecking the orderly formation it had maintained since leaving Pagan, in fact dispersing it to such an extent that Spee temporarily lost sight of half his colliers.

---

3   From Pochhammer, *Before Jutland*. See my methodological Afterword.

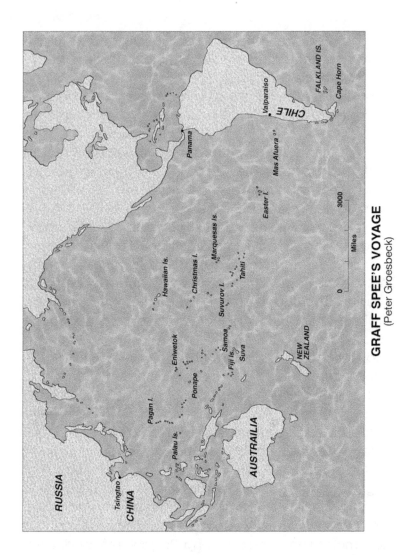

GRAFF SPEE'S VOYAGE
(Peter Groesbeck)

For three days the storm attacked the ships, playing havoc with the smaller steamships and *Nürnberg*, rolling them forty degrees to the brink of capsizing. Everything was wet. The crews had not a dry stitch left on them, nor any dry clothes in their lockers. Nothing stayed in one place unless tied down. Luckily the smaller vessels did not founder, but much of the coal mounded on deck washed overboard along with many of the pigs, sheep, and cattle that we had penned up on deck as a reserve food source. With thousands of miles between our position and Chile, these losses caused great worry.

· · ·

After a wardroom dinner with Fielitz, Pfahl, and other officers of *Scharnhorst*, Graf Spee checked with first officer Heinrich Bender on the storm-tossed bridge: "*Alles in Ordnung?*"

"Yes sir, everything in order. The storm makes it difficult, but no enemy in sight, nothing to report."

"Good. Keep a sharp eye out."

The admiral repaired to his cabin to write a letter to his wife, Countess von Spee. He had not seen Margarete or their ancestral estate since 1912. Separation from a loved one, combined with many stressful days considering unattractive operational options, and on top of this the tension and unrelenting anxiety of the first four days of an especially bad-weather cruise, had clearly taxed him.

Since early July, when war had looked more certain, other signs of apparent misfortune had built up the level of anxiety in his frayed nerves like steam pressure rising in a faulty boiler. For years Germany had planned to deploy an overseas "Flying Division" of powerful battleships to threaten enemy interests in the world if war should suddenly break out. The idea of such a squadron was the hobby horse of Prince Heinrich, the Kaiser's younger brother, twice commander of the East Asiatic (1899-1900) and onetime commander-in-chief of the High Seas Fleet (1906-1909). He opposed the anti-English bent of Tirpitz's expensive concentration of dreadnoughts at Wilhelmshaven and Kiel, favoring instead an English-friendly foreign and naval policy. Prince Heinrich was not so naïve as to rule out the possibility of war with Britain, but thought it wiser in that event to always have a portion of the fleet abroad to challenge the British Empire as opposed to what he considered the outright folly of a North Sea clash.

Heinrich and his faction at naval command did not always get the Kaiser's ear—no one could—but in 1912/1913 they registered some success with deployment of Germany's intimidating new battle cruisers, *Goeben* and *Moltke*, each boasting ten 11-inch and twelve 6-inch guns, four 20-inch torpedo tubes, and superior 28-knot speed despite an armor belt thicker than their British counterparts. The former became flagship of the empire's Mediterranean squadron, performing so well that admiralty decided to reinforce the East Asiatic in early 1914 with a new flagship, *Moltke*. Tirpitz advised against both decisions, but Wilhelm ignored him. The irate naval minister was not greatly consoled by the postponement of *Moltke*'s transfer to the Far East until *Goeben* returned home and completed engine overhauls. The outbreak of war interrupted both moves.

Another sign that the royal younger brother was making headway with his agenda came in late 1913 when the forerunner of the Flying Division, the so-called Detached Division, put to sea, visiting West Africa that winter and both coasts of South America in the spring, Prince Heinrich rendezvousing with the Division in Valparaiso before all sailed back to the Fatherland in mid-June 1914. The Detached Division consisted of two of the newest and fastest dreadnought battleships, *Kaiser* and *König Albert*, and one of the newest light cruisers, *Strassburg*.

Somewhat reluctantly, Tirpitz decided in early 1914 to upstage the Prince and bring the Flying Division into being. Although still complaining—correctly—about the penchant of his political enemies to over-estimate Britain's desire for peace with Germany, and threatening to resign if the Kaiser insisted on funding for an additional four light cruisers for *guerre de course* in the Mediterranean, he nevertheless readied a budget proposal to place in commission abroad a division of four battleships—an imposing squadron of dreadnoughts somewhere in the world, should war erupt, to create instant headaches for the English.

Of course, none of the best-laid but largely unimplemented plans of Prince Heinrich and Tirpitz could help—or improve spirits aboard—the marooned ships of the East Asiatic. "If only we had warships here with more fighting power!" bemoaned Captain Schönberg of *Nürnberg*. "There is nothing to do but think, and that is not good," lamented Maerker, full of doubt and depression about the odds they faced. One of his lieutenant commanders who thought too much, Joachim Lietzmann, worried that those irreplaceable shells would some day run out in a losing battle: "Many dogs will be the death of the hare if this war lasts long enough. That is clear to everyone and no one believes we'll see home again." A fatalistic "twilight of the gods" mood reigned in the squadron, noted Schönberg, even with Graf Spee, whom he labeled "the loneliest man in the world."

A lonely man, a lonely squadron, a need for ships with more fighting power—these thoughts must have weighed on the chief's mind this stormy August day. He knew he probably would not be getting *Moltke*— not right away, anyway, maybe later?—but surely Graf Spee, a protégé of Prince Heinrich, wondered just a little more about the whereabouts of the Detached Division. He had to have asked himself if these ships had put to sea again before the declaration of war. Six weeks was certainly ample time. Indeed it was tantalizingly tempting to consider how much greater the squadron's chances of survival when reaching Chile would be if they spotted, bristling in harbor there, the mighty guns and thick armor belts of *Kaiser* and *König Albert*—twenty 12-inch guns for Churchill to think about! Because all ships of the squadron maintained radio silence, no inquiries could be made, but why was there no wireless from Berlin?!

As he dipped his pen for ink, Graf Spee tried to suppress these weak-moment thoughts. If, evidently, one battle cruiser and the two battleships of the Detached Division represented so significant a reinforcement of the home fleet that they had to stay behind at home, this only strengthened the Count's desire to bring his ships back to Germany too. He began to write, but his mood remained dark and foreboding:

*"Pacific Ocean, near the Marshall   August 18th 1914
Islands*

The English, French, and Russian squadrons have united against us. The East Asiatic, inferior in strength, can do nothing against them. The English also have an Australian squadron lurking with battle cruiser Australia as flagship. This ship alone is so superior to my entire squadron that I have no choice but to flee her. Given this unfavorable balance of power do not expect us to perform great deeds.

But in these vast open waters it will not be easy to find us—as long as our coal holds out. So far, thank God, luck favors us. We all lead a very monotonous life, however. In the evenings no lights, such that nights last a full twelve hours.

The great suffering that war brings in its wake, suffering that will touch many, is unimportant when compared to the fate of the world that will be decided in this great struggle. There is no doubt that the German people will fight bravely.

As for me, it is strange how unimportant I feel when I think of what is at stake in this titanic clash of mighty empires, and how little I personally value my life. For me the coming of war, however it may turn out, brought a release of all the pre-war tension. I would willingly give my life in the service of the Fatherland. I can face with good conscience everything that the future brings, come what may, for, to be frank, in the grand scheme of passing time everything passes, everything disappears."

Graf Spee's words to home were not normal for a man facing the distinct possibility of imminent death in combat. Usually men in harm's way paint positive pictures for loved ones lest badly chosen words alarm family back home. But this letter, which bordered on the macabre, had another purpose, one he hoped she would understand.

Graf Maximilian von Spee: Worst-will-happen-fatalist
(Kirchoff, *Maximilian Graf von Spee*)

He planned to detach *Nürnberg* to Hawaii once they reached Eniwetok. His light cruiser would inform the German consulate of the squadron's plan to round the Horn and return home, and also deliver letters to Germany from all the ships' companies. Given the squadron's predicament, all of these letters could very well be the men's last letters—and his too. Graf Spee wanted to say goodbye in a way to assuage Margarete's grief and anguish by planting the thought that he had not been anxious or afraid, that he had not suffered, that he had died honorably, and that she should be proud of him. (The letter reached her hands in early October).

Having read over what he had written, Graf Spee looked somewhat pleased. But a tired, furrowed brow belied any feeling of satisfaction, an unmistakable sign that the fatalism so common to Germans had begun to overtake him—a "the-worst-will-happen-but-come-what-may" fatalism that was very much a character trait of his too. As a commander he wanted to win great victories and bring his men through, as a father he wanted to protect his sons, and as a husband he wanted to be with his wife again. The fault lines of this fatalistic fissure in Graf Spee's mental makeup had widened, however, threatening to suck him into the crevasse of rash and ill-conceived actions.

• • •

Midday on August 18th the battering finally eased. Now intense heat and sunshine once again converted our ships to sweaty steam baths. On the 19th the atoll of Eniwetok finally came into view, first the green of tall palm trees, then the white sand of the beaches. All crews were exhausted but could expect no rest, for after dropping anchors the physical challenge of coaling began anew. Before nightfall every ship was a black, dusty, filthy mess. The dirty work continued on August 20th.

• • •

While the coaling proceeded, Spee convened his captains and first officers for a leisurely luncheon in the wardroom of his cleanest ship, *Prince Eitel Friedrich*. After the stewards had cleared the tables, the company played a few rubbers of bridge.

At one table Spee and Maerker took on the first officers of the heavy cruisers, Heinrich Bender and Hans Pochhammer, whose side won unexpectedly—a surprise because the two older friends were the best at bridge in the squadron. Spee showed his usual aggressive style, playing his cards as if giving orders in battle. But he made some obvious mistakes that surprised Maerker, and amused Pochhammer, who tried some humor: "Fortunes of war, sir, fortunes of war."

Having lost, the admiral was not in the mood to laugh. Rather, he cast one of his notorious "thunderbolt" glances at the now contrite Pochhammer. Then, gathering himself together, he responded more gracefully to the junior man. "You're quite right, Pochhammer. When the day of reckoning comes I trust ships' officers will perform better *on* the bridge than I have *at* bridge today."

Standing up, he spoke to the group: "Gentlemen, finish up, then I'll start the briefing."

• • •

Our admiral unfolded a large chart of the Pacific and began to explain his plans, this time, unlike the conference on Pagan, allowing for no discussion. He poked at the different sites on the map as he told us that *Nürnberg* would be detached to Honolulu to establish contact with the Admiralty, rejoining the squadron at

Christmas Island, that agents in North and South America would procure coal and supplies for us when we reached Chile, that *Leipzig*, and from the Caribbean, hopefully, light cruiser *Dresden* too, would receive orders to rendezvous with us at Easter Island, that as we neared Chile we must soon face combat with the English, who would never tolerate an interruption of their vital trade in nitrates with South America lest it disrupt the manufacture of explosives, that we would round Cape Horn, and, who could tell, perhaps, against all the odds, fight our way through the Atlantic to Germany.

"If we sail over the Caribbean," he said, "light cruiser *Karlsruhe* can reinforce us. However gentlemen, long before this we could encounter serious opposition—a flotilla more powerful than the East Asiatic. At least the enemy would have been forced to commit a significant portion of his fleet in finding us. But I need not tell you what it would mean to the Fatherland if two heavy and five light cruisers, seven warships manned by seasoned crews and crack gunners, all armed with deadly torpedoes and mines, manage to reunite with the home fleet. At any point of our homebound cruise Admiralty may detach capital ships to assist us, or, if we make it close enough to Europe, send the whole fleet out. If and when that day comes we will defeat the English and gain control of the North Sea, however many of us pay with our lives. But our sacrifice means the difference between defeat and victory in this great world war—or in the next."

The thought of being home warmed our hearts, but Graf Spee's not so thinly veiled pessimism about our chances generated anxiety among us.

X
SAMOA AND PAPEETE

We left Eniwetok on August 22nd, detaching *Nürnberg* that same day. The heavy cruisers and colliers crept slowly toward Christmas Island to preserve fuel.

Every day it seemed we were called to battle stations for what turned out to be a false alarm—the enemy had still not been sighted. Day after day passed, the sun baking the ships and making life unbearable below decks. Officers at least had port holes to open for breeze at night, but because we steamed blacked out, it meant lying in a darkened room, alone with your thoughts, apprehensions assuming exaggerated proportions, as is usual at night. It was all quite dispiriting. We had been trained to think we were the best at our game—"take us on at your own risk"—but here we were, hiding, hoping not to be found, just running away.

On Sunday, September 6th, we lay at anchor in the small cove of an uninhabited island not far from Christmas Island. After church services various teams had been sent ashore to search for fresh water and fruit. Suddenly, lookouts spotted a speck of smoke far to the north. In automatic unison both vulnerable warships raised all possible steam, hove to, and hurried out to confront the intruder. As so often in past days bells sounded battle stations, the crews manned guns, and magazine handlers elevated shells to the gun turrets and casemates.

After a half hour, however, our anxiety turned miraculously to joy: the approaching warship flew German ensigns—she was the *Nürnberg* returning from sea. We all rejoiced. The East Asiatic was now stronger—three ships, not two—and we were relieved that four hundred comrades had avoided a terrible fate: mass death at sea. We also felt the inward happiness of our admiral. We all had families, some of us, like Schönberg and I, wives and children, but our families were safe in the Fatherland—at least so we hoped—but Graf Spee's son, Otto, served as an ensign aboard the returning *Nürnberg*. His other son, Heinrich, served on *Gneisenau*.

• • •

On September 7th the fugitive flotilla entered the bay of Christmas Island. Once at anchor, *Nürnberg*'s launch brought its captain to the flagship to report. He was piped aboard and shown to Spee's suite.

"Welcome back to the squadron, Schönberg. Thanks to God for granting us this reunion. Now, captain, please tell me about your voyage. Did you learn anything about enemy dispositions?"

"We sighted no British or Japanese ships the entire time. But sir, I am pleased to report that we struck a blow against the enemy. Per your orders I put a landing party ashore on Fanning Island and destroyed a British wireless station and telegraph cable. It was a minor victory, but this first action did wonders for the morale of ship's company after weeks of inaction and mounting anxiety. Sir, I also bring newspapers from Honolulu. There's important news, which I'd like …"

"Is there anything in the papers about German dreadnoughts on the high seas?

"Nothing sir, although I—all of us—hope Admiralty still intends to reinforce us."

Graf Spee nodded but said nothing, leaving his own hopes to himself.

"But there is something else, sir—not good news I'm afraid. An expedition from Australia and New Zealand, spearheaded, it appears, by *Australia*, landed at Apia and seized German Samoa nine days ago."

Spee stood up, walked over to his huge wall map, and put his finger on Samoa. "So … *Australia* at Apia."

He paused to think, hand on chin. "What do you think, Schönberg, could she still be there?"

"It's quite possible admiral, especially if the enemy suspects you are in nearby waters."

"We just might be, captain, we just might be," said Spee, a serious kind of smile slowly coming to his face. "I want Schultz and Maerker to join us in an hour. You wait here with me. Let's take a look at these newspapers. What's going on in Europe? Has Paris fallen?"

"Our armies have crossed the Marne River, admiral. Victory on the Western Front must be near!"

• • •

Within the hour Spee's three captains sat at his conference table. "Gentlemen, be seated. Let me lay out a plan for our first action."

The admiral explained a risky operation that had come quickly into his mind while talking with Schönberg. The morale of the men needed a boost, and dramatic action for the squadron, especially for the crews of the heavy cruisers, would provide just that. He had to consider every opportunity to inflict harm on the enemy, moreover, and catching *Australia* vulnerable at anchor with no steam up, and perhaps also trapping *Minotaur* or *Hampshire* or light cruisers *Yarmouth* or *Sydney*, would be a coup for the Imperial German Navy and the Fatherland. So he intended to reverse course, steam the heavy cruisers without colliers to impede them south-southwest to Samoa, a five day voyage, and then pounce upon enemy ships at first light.

When he had finished, he said, as was fairly customary with him: "What is your view of the situation, gentlemen?"

"May I play devil's advocate, Max?" ventured Maerker.

"Yes, of course Gustav."

"If we cruise at high speed 1,500 miles to Samoa, consuming vast amounts of coal, and then find the harbor empty, we will have delayed our arrival off Chile by two weeks and perhaps have jeopardized our agreed-upon goal of making successfully for home, all to no avail. If, on the other hand, the enemy is using Apia as a base for hunting us down, he will have light cruiser patrols out, perhaps the whole flotilla out looking for us in Samoan waters. This could be the end of us."

The admiral gave his answer without hesitation: "I am quite prepared to take these risks."

As there did not seem to be any reason to continue the discussion after Spee's emphatic remark, which signaled that he had already made up his mind, the table fell silent. Both Maerker and Schultz looked apprehensive, especially Maerker, who frowned but did not push his point further out of respect for friendship as well as military discipline.

The captain's thoughts, however, were anything but positive: "*He* is prepared for the risks?! And the deaths of 1,600 men?! And our never seeing the Fatherland again?!"

"Very well then," said Graf Spee, "bring coal aboard tomorrow and have steam up for departure at 0600 on the 9th."

• • •

Our heavy cruisers, coal heaped in every conceivable spot on deck, weighed anchor and steamed southwest. The old salts knew that some action beckoned—there could be no other explanation for five days in a row of gunnery and simulated combat drills. Having been briefed, the officers, of course, were keenly aware that very soon the East Asiatic Squadron's big guns would be more than mere mute witnesses, as they had been thus far, to the war that raged in the world.[4]

Debates raged in the wardrooms, too, as the 9th of September slowly yielded to the 13th. Most officers believed that a distinguished destiny awaited *Scharnhorst* and *Gneisenau* in the harbor at Apia. Ships named after two of Germany's most heroic generals of the Napoleonic Wars would surely mete out hard knocks to an enemy that had betrayed the Fatherland with his perfidious declaration of war. Although as first officer I knew about Captain Maerker's doubts and worries, I kept such thoughts to myself during these heated discussions. Whatever lay in that harbor, it seemed better to agree with the hotheads in order to keep their martial ardor well-stoked.

As darkness enveloped our two awesome vessels late on the evening of September 13th, the former German colony of West Samoa lay only a hundred nautical miles farther to the south. That night the officers and crew changed into clean uniforms. If wounds were to be inflicted on the morn, cleanliness meant some guard against infection. At 0500 on September 14th Maerker ordered us to battle stations. Around our necks dangled gauze masks, a precursor of the gas mask, as well as a red silk ID tag—to identify the dead.

When I came on deck it was still a wonderful tropical night, pitch black on the water, above us a resplendent sky lit by stars and a crescent moon. The men stood about the deck in groups, shivering in the predawn chill. Here and there a pipe was puffing—a last

---

4   From Pochhammer, *Before Jutland*. See my methodological Afterword.

comfort before blood was shed, or a calming check to the emotions that surged in each one of us.

After an hour it became lighter. We knew that very soon a blood-red sun would rise out of the eastern sea. As *Gneisenau* and *Scharnhorst* reached full speed, rushing toward the harbor with battle ensigns flying proudly, water spraying menacingly over our bows, details began to emerge from the still distant, still darkened mass of land. A thin white line of coral rocks marked the coast. Behind a low-lying peninsula jutting out to sea, brighter streaks and spots probably revealed the town of Apia. Or were these lights from vessels in the inner harbor? We strained our eyes to see funnels, masts, and gun turrets. We braced ourselves to meet what fate had in store.

But destiny disappointed. When the sun rose we saw only the beautiful palm-covered slopes of the colony we knew so well, its volcanic range rising 4,000 feet above us. The harbor was completely empty—no *Australia*, no *Minotaur*, no *Yarmouth* or *Sydney*, not even a little gunboat or merchant steamer.

Hearts sank, but we also relaxed in the knowledge that no one would die this day. My captain summed up the relief as well as the frustration in one sentence: "I live, we live, and *they live too*," said Maerker.

· · ·

Seeing the empty harbor from the bridge of his flagship, the admiral lowered his binoculars, the look of a gambler who had played and lost coming over his face. Spee stared straight ahead. "My Lord, why have you forsaken me?" he half-thought, half-mumbled, lips barely moving. Then he collected himself, straightening up even more erect than usual, and said, still staring ahead: "What will be, will be."

A moment of silence later he finally turned toward Schultz with new orders. "Turn about and steady her on northwest. After nightfall, head due east. They weren't foolish enough to be caught at anchor, but perhaps this old ruse will fool them into thinking we're steaming back to Eniwetok."

All day long and into the evening the German heavy cruisers stayed their course, losing more time and consuming more coal—much more of both than Spee had anticipated when he left Christmas Island. During this 120-mile trek the radio room of *Scharnhorst* picked up a wireless message from Apia: "Enemy ships disappearing in a northwesterly direction." The ruse was working. Finally after nightfall they turned back to the east.

Another 2,500 miles and another ten days would bring them to the Marquesas Islands, far to the southeast of Christmas Island, for the appointed rendezvous with *Nürnberg* and the colliers. One of the squadron's fuel ships, the *Ahlers*, waited for the cruisers a few days to the east of Samoa at the Suvurov atoll.

·   ·   ·

Still eager to have action, and determined to contribute in some way to Germany's war effort, Spee steered a little farther than necessary to the southeast, for here lay the French Tahiti Islands, where he might conduct a successful raid, do some damage, take aboard food and water, and perhaps rake these colonies of their coal supplies.

On September 21st the would-be raiders stopped at Bora-Bora. Because the inhabitants remained oblivious to the world's war, the squadron purchased provisions and stored them away. The next day, however, would bring the ships to Papeete, the administrative capital of Tahiti, a port guarded by an antiquated but still very dangerous fort. Destruction of this citadel and seizure of the island's rich coal stores would in some small way begin to justify the empire's investment of men and money in its East Asiatic Squadron, and for Spee, justify his entire *raison d'etre*, even if it meant his death. These thoughts twisted around in the mind of this troubled man.

Maerker once again advised against the operation, which meant trying to maneuver in cramped harbor waters. He was overruled, however, by Graf Spee, whose head had been turned, Maerker thought, by second staff officer Pfahl, an "evil spirit" who "just absolutely wants to see blood." But what could the captain of *Gneisenau* do? "I can only hope that all turns out well. I have to obey even if my advice is not heard."

An hour after first light on September 22nd—the same day *Emden* bombarded Madras—*Scharnhorst* and *Gneisenau* entered the harbor of Papeete and got within 9,000 yards of shore. Suddenly, white puffs from the hillside fort were observed on both ships' bridges. Alerted by the British Admiralty after the Samoan incident, the French Colonial Office had put all stations in the South Central Pacific on alert. The shore battery on

Papeete, consisting of eight older 6-inch cannon, had fired on *Scharnhorst* when she came within range. The well-aimed shots fell in a tight pattern, straddling the cruiser only fifty yards to port and starboard.

Alarmed for the safety of his ships, Spee immediately cast a thunderbolt glance at Schultz, who had already ordered a sharp turn to port to steer full-line ahead, thereby presenting a smaller target as they neared the fort. On the bridge of *Gneisenau*, Maerker had quickly veered to port too.

The tactical situation still favored the land battery—from close range a flat trajectory naval shot had to strike a direct hit on a small one-cannon target, or fly harmlessly overhead, while forts' guns arced down on a huge mass of metal—but the East Asiatic's gunnery was legendary in the Imperial German Navy. The first salvos, fired from much closer range, scored four direct hits and sent the gun crews of the fort into a panicky rush for cover. Two more broadsides had reduced the rampart to a heap of burning, smoking rubble.

A French gunboat that had bravely charged from its mooring to do battle, firing off a few rounds from its 4.0- and 2.5-inch guns, was blown violently apart and sunk in seconds, killing the entire crew of twenty-five men. "Looked like murderous holocaust," Maerker wrote later—"it was terrible!" "What impudence," exclaimed a much more battle-ramped Pochhammer, "to open fire on us with a couple of pea shooters!" Many among the German crews exuded the same arrogantly, angrily proud emotions. The first blood had been spilled—and it was not theirs.

Here, at least, was something they could show the Fatherland. And now, at least, the crews' morale had been lifted. But Spee was again prevented from achieving all operational goals, for, much to his chagrin, the admiral spotted black smoke clouds enveloping the island, which meant that all coal stocks had been set ablaze.

Only one recourse remained: turn about, proceed eastwards for several days to the Marquesas and a reunion with *Nürnberg*, and then on and on, farther and farther and farther to the southeast, across the equator and all the way to Easter Island, where, hopefully, *Leipzig* and *Dresden* would be waiting.

XI
EASTER ISLAND

Our three warships took on water, provisions, and coal for an entire week before setting a course for Easter Island, more than 2,500 miles away, on October 2nd. Once again the cruisers steamed in line to port, the colliers to starboard. Two of the flotilla's steamers, now empty of their indispensable cargo, Graf Spee sent to Hawaii.

Prince Eitel Friedrich no longer led the coal ships. She had been detached from the Marshall Islands for solo surface raiding. Her daring Captain Thiereken eventually sank twelve enemy merchant ships off Latin America before running low on coal and putting into Newport News, Virginia, where she was interned by the United States. In nearby seas light cruiser *Karlsruhe* also ran up the score against British commerce, sinking or capturing eighteen ships before her ammunition overheated on Barbados later that autumn, explosively terminating operations for the *Emden* of the Caribbean. Graf Spee was never to learn the fate of these two ships.

During the first night out from the Marquesas the wireless rooms of the big cruisers picked up a staccato-like "Dr, Dr, Dr," call sign of SMS *Dresden*. She lay off the coast of Chile, having rounded Cape Horn three weeks earlier. She had orders for SMS *Leipzig*, steaming somewhere to the north.

Our radiomen heard no reply from *Leipzig*, but two nights later, October 4th-5th, they again picked up signals from the southerly ship: "My position 31.25 south, 89.58 west, near Más Afuera, 500 miles west Valparaiso. Have contacted *Leipzig* with Admiralty orders to reinforce cruiser squadron at Easter Island."

For the first time on his long voyage our admiral decided to break radio silence so as to coordinate the reunion with the long-absent *Leipzig* and the newest addition to the East Asiatic, *Dresden*, comparable in design to our newest, fastest cruiser, *Emden*. Soon enough the radio room heard "Le, Le, Le," *Leipzig*'s call sign.

On October 13th, when *Scharnhorst*, *Gneisenau*, and *Nürnberg* finally reached the remote island with its stone faces staring, according to legend, mutely and morosely out to sea, *Dresden* already lay at anchor with her collier to port. The next day *Leipzig* and three additional colliers arrived. Despite detaching *Emden* the squadron had gotten up to full-strength.

Newspapers brought from Peru by *Leipzig* contained a mix of good news along with more cause for anxiety. We read with pride about *Emden*'s string of fourteen sinkings and captures and her bombardment of Madras. On the other hand, this news was over two weeks old. Was Captain Müller's raider still afloat? The other less than consoling side of things was that *Dresden*'s orders from Berlin contained nothing about either *Moltke* or the Detached Division on which our admiral had still placed some hope. There could be no doubt now that the East Asiatic was on its own—we had gotten a double reinforcement to end our loneliness, but we were still vulnerably, nerve-wrenchingly alone.

We had steamed over 8,000 miles from Pagan Island, however, remarkably covering more than a third of the distance to Germany. *Leipzig*, which had seized or sunk three enemy merchant ships underway, had made the long voyage from San Francisco, and *Dresden* had come farther than any of them, having started in the Caribbean. She had seized or sunk four merchantmen on this cruise. Valparaiso, where the admiral anticipated taking on ample coal supplies and other provisions, lay nearly 3,000 miles farther east.

• • •

Underway from the Marquesas the weather had turned colder as each southeasterly mile put the German fugitives farther and farther into the still-wintry southern hemisphere. They locked away their white summer uniforms and got out blue cold weather gear.

Not long after reaching Easter Island, Spee and his elder son, Otto, an officer aboard *Nürnberg*, boarded a launch and went ashore to see the huge monolithic statues, most having toppled over centuries ago. Father and son stood in a heavy, nearly freezing rain, umbrellas only partially shielding them from the windswept downpour. Evidently preoccupied, Spee had said little since leaving the ship.

Otto, too, fixed his thoughts more on the present than on the Stone-Age past. "Everyone says we will see action soon. It's the only topic of conversation in the wardroom. It seems English men-of-war pursued *Dresden* around the Cape."

Spee thought briefly about keeping what he knew to himself, but then, assuming this information would soon be made known in officers' briefings, decided to answer forthrightly. "Yes, Otto, we're fortunate to have received fairly detailed intelligence from our agents in South America about what may soon be steaming our way. We're researching their capabilities as we speak: an old battleship with 12-inch guns, two outdated cruisers, and a newer light cruiser. The last one worries me a bit. With its speed and 6-inch guns, our light cruisers are outmatched, but of course we have three to their one. The rest we can deal with."

Spee walked over to one of the ancient gods, almost completely sunk in the mud of myriad rains, and put his foot up on it. "Don't worry, son, we'll grind the English under our heels. They should not have declared war on the Fatherland. It gives me no pleasure to think about it I can assure you, in fact it pains me, but they'll soon be sunk, like this sad fellow in the muck here."

• • •

Could the warships of the East Asiatic really "deal with" the flotilla London had sent to block their path? In truth, Graf Spee was not at all so cock sure about his chances. He was quite anxious, in fact, about getting past the 12-inch guns of that English battleship. Of course he would do his duty, but he could not do it well if he suppressed an instinct for survival and his love for Margarette, Otto, and Heinrich and charged head-long into battle to "deal with" a superior enemy. Which one, martial fatalism or love of family, would prevail? Without a doubt he would be no coward, but would his inner struggle allow him to think clearly and rationally?

•   •   •

"Do we also know who's in command?" asked Otto.

"No we don't, but *Dresden* was pursued out of the Caribbean by the British West Indies Squadron commanded by Kit Cradock, an old friend of mine from the China station. So maybe it's him at the helm. He's not as unintelligent as some think, and he's brave and fearless. Perhaps we can make these last qualities work to our advantage."

Spee thought about what he had said and shook his head. Then he removed his foot and slipped, but did not fall. "Well, enough of this, Otto, we should return to the squadron."

They walked back to the launch. In the distance the cruisers pitched and rolled at anchor. The storm was getting worse.

•   •   •

Having coaled the entire squadron, taken aboard food and water, and given the crews extra days to rest, our small fleet was ready to leave Easter Island on

Sunday, October 18th. Church services were held that morning aboard all ships, after which, the East Asiatic weighed anchor. The destination of the squadron, Más Afuera, lay well over 2,000 miles to the east.

XII
LONDON

If the map of the world in Spee's suite was large, that in the War Room of the British Admiralty in London was huge. Twenty feet high and thirty feet wide, it occupied the entire wall. On October 5th First Lord of the Admiralty Winston Churchill caucused there with First Sea Lord Louis Mountbatten, his chief of staff, Vice-Admiral Frederick Doveton Sturdee, and Far East theater expert Admiral Sir Henry Jackson. All worried about the safety of the world's largest merchant marine, which German surface raiders in only two months of war had reduced in size by two percent.

For the past thirty days confusion had reigned in the Admiralty. The exact whereabouts of *Emden* or even the remote position of Spee and the rest of the German East Asiatic Squadron were unknown. The king's navy had also failed to prevent *Dresden* from escaping the Caribbean, nor could it find *Karlsruhe*. Potentially just as bad, *Königsberg* had not been located despite sinking the first British merchant ship of the war, *City of Winchester*, and appearing boldly on the Royal Navy's doorstep in Zanzibar and destroying two warships. Admiralty guessed that she hid in the Rufigi River Delta of German East Africa, but this was not certain.

The cats were already way ahead in this high stakes cat and mouse game, but what if *Königsberg* broke out to join the hunt?

The biggest threat to commerce remained *Emden*, which by this time had shelled Madras and sunk or captured fourteen ships. Her total would soon rise to twenty-one. Worse still, hundreds of ship captains in the ports that rimmed the Indian Ocean refused to put to sea, thus greatly magnifying the significant damage done by the German corsair. Adding to the alarm, the public in Australia and New Zealand, where convoys for the ANZAC corps were ready to sail for Suez, demanded that the Royal Navy sink the enemy raider before their boys embarked.

• • •

This day Churchill was beside himself. "I wish to point out to you most clearly," he barked at Jackson, who stood next to him at the wall map, "that the irritation in the Far East caused by the continuing captures of the *Emden* is doing great damage to the Admiralty's reputation! India is nervous and sticky!" Mountbatten and Sturdee, standing on the other side of the First Lord, nodded in approval.

But before Jackson could reply, Churchill barreled forward, his voice rising, his right arm thrusting at the map sites. "I am quite at a loss to understand the efforts of *Hampshire*'s captain to catch the *Emden*. Who is this captain? Is he good? Ten days ago he headed into the eastern Bay of Bengal, but one day later we reported *Emden* steaming south from Ceylon. Didn't *Hampshire* get this information? And what has happened to the light cruiser *Yarmouth*? She's modern, fast, and has *Emden* badly outgunned, but her movements appear to be entirely disjointed and purposeless. We must take measures without further delay which will give reasonable promise of decisive results. Only when we have cruiser sweeps of eight to ten vessels ten to fifteen miles apart will we achieve those results!"

• • •

By the middle of September the Admiralty had heard nothing of the core of the East Asiatic Squadron since Spee's heavy cruisers had shown the flag in Ponapé in the German Carolines on August 8th. Since then Jackson had done an in-depth study of the German's likely strategy, concluding that since he had not yet attacked Hong Kong it meant he was probably attempting to reach Chile and raid commerce there, but this intelligence report was called seriously into question by Spee's appearance in the harbor at Samoa on September 14th. The raid misfired, but at least the ruse of steaming away to the northwest had worked brilliantly, for Churchill ordered his squadrons in the Far East to search the Marshall Islands, where it appeared Spee had sailed.

When he hit Papeete eight days later, however, Churchill changed orders a second time, for Spee might strike west to Samoa again, farther southwest to Fiji, or even all the way to New Zealand. Not until October 5th, a few hours after Spee broke radio silence, could Admiralty confirm Jackson's theory: the East

Asiatic indeed sailed for Chile, intending first to rendez-vous on Easter Island, but London lacked intelligence on the exact number of light cruisers Spee had with him.

• • •

"As for Spee," Churchill said to Jackson, having calmed himself down a bit, "you were right all along, at least according to the information we received today. He certainly has sailed a long way, but that will be his undoing. He's cut off from his base at Tsingtao, and so has no means to dock his ships, execute serious repairs and maintenance, and replenish his magazines. And now that he has left the German Pacific islands behind, his coal will soon run low—that he has gotten this far is impressive, but he is like a cut flower in a vase: fair to see, yet bound to die, and to die very soon if the water in the vase is not constantly renewed."

Turning to Mountbatten, Churchill asked: "What ships have we got in the South Atlantic to block Spee's path?"

"Admiral Cradock has moved south in his pursuit of *Dresden*, but she appears to have eluded him. Based in the Falklands, where we ordered him three weeks ago, he has an old county class cruiser, *Monmouth*, with 6-inch ordnance, an even older armored cruiser, *Good Hope*, with two 9.2-inch guns, and the newer light cruiser *Glasgow*, with 6-inch guns. He also has *Ortanto*, a liner converted to auxiliary cruiser that will provide some flexibility with reconnaissance and against German merchantmen. To assure that Spee is outclassed I propose to shift *Minotaur*'s sister ship, HMS *Defence*, from the Mediterranean to join Cradock's command. We expect the Turks to ally soon with Germany—as you know, battle cruiser *Goeben* has already escaped through the Dardanelles to join them—but despite this we have more than adequate force left there to deal with them."

"Gentlemen," interjected Sturdee, "if we're serious about stopping Von Spee we should send battle cruisers. I've raised this point before and wish to reiterate it."

Churchill wasn't buying it. "No dreadnoughts or battle cruisers can be spared from the Grand Fleet at Scapa Flow or the battle cruiser squadron at Cromarty Firth, Sturdee. But you're right that we need more strength. Is an older battleship available?"

"Cradock is thinking along the same lines," said Mountbatten. "He has ordered HMS *Canopus* to steam south from the Cape Verde Islands to Port Stanley. She's a fifteen-year old queen class battleship, but boasts four 12-inch guns and has decent speed."

"Excellent," said Churchill, who thought for a moment and then continued. "Yes, of course, *Scharnhorst* and *Gneisenau* will never venture voluntarily within decisive range of *Canopus* and subject themselves to very serious damage. This grand old ship with her heavy armor and artillery will be a citadel around which all our cruisers in those waters will find absolute security. And perhaps with luck we can entice Spee into a trap and destroy this menace to the British Empire."

Churchill paused, looking quite confident and proud of himself. "Is there anything else gentlemen?"

As there was not, he had to hurry off to a meeting of the War Cabinet.

XIII
PORT STANLEY AND VALPARAISO

Rear Admiral Sir Christopher Cradock, called simply "Kit" by his friends, was one year younger than the German he had orders to find and destroy, but started his naval career two years earlier as a thirteen-year old cadet in 1875. With a larger overseas empire, Britain offered her sailors better opportunity to test their mettle in battle, and so Cradock had also seen more action: in Africa, the Middle East, and the Far East. He had met and befriended Maximilian von Spee in China while helping other European nations suppress the Boxer Rebellion in 1900.

Cradock never married. As a single man he devoted much spare time to writing and, impressively enough, had three books to his name and also dabbled in poetry. Although he certainly had a cerebral side, this was usually lost on those who knew him only casually or observed him from a distance. To them he seemed a brave, hot-headed, rather simple seaman who "fought hard and played hard and did not suffer fools gladly," as one fellow captain remembered him. Although Cradock had said that "a captain's ship must never race faster than his brain," his favorite order from the bridge was nevertheless that of Lord Nelson at Trafalgar: "Engage the enemy more closely." When the forty-year veteran of the Royal Navy came face to face with Spee, which side would predominate, the cautious, think-it-through-first, or the impetuous, charge-first, ask-questions-later?

Christopher Cradock: "Engage the enemy more closely"
(Imperial War Museum)

• • •

Lloyd Higgs, one of the veteran officers aboard HMS *Glasgow*, leaned on a portside railing. Far off to the north East Falkland Island was just coming into view through a misty, low-lying cloud bank. He puffed on a pipe and began to smile as land drew closer and closer. A gust of salty sea wind nearly blew off his cap, but left his smile. Something warm and endearing must have been waiting inside the cold of the Falklands, a cold that usually cut to the quick.

• • •

In the last days of September my light cruiser, His Majesty's Ship *Glasgow*, along with the rest of our squadron, having searched unsuccessfully for the elusive *Dresden* in the inlets and harbors off the Magellan Straits, returned to Port Stanley to coal. On Thursday, October 1st, we rounded Cape Pembroke lighthouse, steamed through Port William, the outer harbor, and then into innermost Stanley Harbor.

East Falkland Island, which houses the port, presented a bleak picture to our tired sailors. Nary a tree could be seen, nor did epidemics break out because, as we used to joke, the continuous westerly gales had blown away all the bugs.[5] Only the Anglican cathedral most familiar to me, a Presbyterian church, Government House, dockside cranes and warehouses, and the masts of the whalers and sealers marked the horizon. Barren, desolate, and wind-swept, the place was

---

5   From Hickling, *Sailor at Sea*. See my methodological Afterword.

fit for none but sea lions, seals, penguins, albatrosses, and a few thousand rugged descendants of the Scandinavian whalers and Scottish sheep farmers who had settled here since we acquired the Falklands in the 1830s.

Even though East Falkland looked like a moonscape, it still cheered our hearts. The people of the island treated us well—they shared their simple lives with us. Every officer and man had his "up home" where he was taken in and welcomed as one of the family.

At first sight of our flotilla, the older daughters of the sheep herders rode into town with party frocks stowed in their saddle bags and made ready to greet and meet at the town's two raucous pubs, "The Stanley Arms" and "The Rose and Crown." The beer there was potent, as many a sailor found to his undoing—it had to be fortified in order to stand the long trip through the tropics from Britain. The hardy maidens waited largely in vain, for Cradock had issued orders to start the coaling immediately—no shore leave for the men on this trip. Not so for some of the other officers and I who got shore leave and escaped overseeing the dirty business. Most of my mates headed for the pubs—we had come to think of them as *our* pubs over the last few years. I had other plans.

● ● ●

Like Higgs, Kit Cradock also had other plans. He had invited his old friend, Governor of the Falklands Sir William Allardyce, and the governor's *aide de camp*,

Thomas Goddard, to dine in his cabin. The admiral and a constant companion, his aging, loyal Cocker Spaniel, Nelson, greeted them at the door. Cradock had furnished his quarters amply enough for such occasions, but the walls he left bare, undecorated in the Spartan simplicity one would expect of such a martial personality. The only décor, in fact, was a vase of *cloisonné* porcelain whose head, broken off, lay beside it atop a shelf.

"Welcome, lads, drinks all 'round," he trumpeted while pouring glasses full of port wine. "That's it, drink up, drink up, don't peck at it," he ordered as Allardyce and Goddard complied. "Do you good, like mother's milk—Cockburn's Special Reserve 1876!"

After downing their glasses as commanded, the company sat down and engaged in small talk for a few minutes until Allardyce changed to a more important topic. "Kit, do tell us: what's going on with that crafty German admiral from China? Is he coming our way?"

"Admiralty still isn't sure," replied Cradock immediately, "but I've felt all along that my old friend Graf Spee would break for home waters—which probably means passing this way. He welcomes battle, and the biggest battle will be between the British and German fleets back in Europe. He doesn't want to miss the big showdown—of that I'm certain."

Allardyce was about to pose the next obvious question—did Cradock have the ships to do the job against Spee, and started to say this: "What ships has Admiralty given ..." —when he was distracted by the sight of the odd-looking vase. "I do say, Kit, you have unusual taste in porcelain. *Tres chic!*"

"I got it in China when I was a lieutenant and I've carried it with me ever since. It has always brought me luck," replied Cradock. "But last month when on very short notice this became my flagship I only managed to get aboard with my dog in one fist and this vase in the other. I dropped it as soon as I got on *Good Hope* and knocked its head off. I'm very much afraid that that means I'm not going to see these Germans at all."

"I'm sure your luck will hold, Kit. No fox stands a chance when you're in the hunt."

"Quite right, Allardyce. But when fox hunting I always pick my own steed and make certain no one else's mount is a bloody sway-backed, cow-hocked quadruped! I just hope that Admiralty treats me so well, but have you seen what I have to work with so far? Obsolete cruisers too weak to fight, too slow to run away. And if we do get into a scrap, who's to do the fighting? Half-trained reservists, coast guard transfers, and boyish cadets, not regular navy gun layers and veteran old salts. When fox hunting, gentlemen, never dress like a fox."

Cradock's guests looked alarmed. "What are the chances they won't reinforce you, what with Germans on the loose?" said the governor.

"We'll see, we'll see," said the master of grand old *Good Hope* while filling the glasses with more Cockburn '76. "I expect to receive an old battleship, *Canopus*, and a newer armored cruiser, *Defence*. They should move me to the head of the pack."

And then Cradock sought to change the subject. "Tell me, Allardyce, aren't those whaling ships over there?" he observed loudly while pointing out of his port hole. "The hunt for those maritime behemoths must be terribly exciting."

HMS Good Hope: Too weak to fight, too slow to run
(Imperial War Museum)

• • •

Carl Anton Haga managed the South Atlantic operations of the Oslo-based Norwegian Whaling Company. His father, Bjorn Haga, had been captain of one of the firm's vessels that whaled off South Georgia. The industrious son worked his way up, serving aboard his father's ship as a seaman, later in the home office as assistant business manager. By 1882 the company had prospered to the point where it made good business sense to open an office in Port Stanley—South Georgia was at that time largely uninhabited. That same year Haga married the daughter of another whaling captain, the beautiful, intelligent, and feisty Mathilda Steen, and moved to the Falklands to open the office. A daughter came into the world two years later.

This made Anne Mari Haga a "Kelper," island slang, derived from the ubiquitous seaweed of the Falklands, for a native. She was by no means, however, a typical Kelper. As attractive as her mother and just as determined to be independent, this head-turning young Scandinavian graduated from the University of Oslo a year before the war broke out with a degree in education. Along with her native tongue, she spoke fluent Swedish, Danish, English, and German. Shortly after graduation she joined fellow Norwegian women as the first in the world to vote in national elections. She belonged to the International Council of Women, an American-based education and suffrage reform group, was passionate about women everywhere getting the vote, and equally committed to the women's movement's devotion to pacifism and temperance. In short, Anne Mari Haga was a force to be reckoned with, and, despite her outward beauty, few men had tried. In the summer of 1914 the thirty-year-old had returned home to be with her parents, as she had done every summer while at university, and think about career decisions, mainly, whether to teach in Norway or Sweden once the world settled down.

Because there was no Lutheran church in Stanley, the Hagas had begun attending the Anglican Church when it was built in 1892—the service was much closer to the Lutheran than the barebones Presbyterian, which they had not liked. It was here, at a church social in mid-July 1911, that Anne Mari Haga first met Lloyd Higgs of HMS *Glasgow*.

Higgs was dubbed affectionately "Uncle Lloyd" by the younger officers. They called him this for going out of his way to procure all available luxuries in port to make wardroom life more bearable—fresh livestock, cigars, and always a keg of beer or rum. While serving in the South Atlantic, he frequently made port call in the Falklands, enjoying most of all the rowdy bachelor outings to the "Rose and Crown." Half-Irish, half-English, he was fond of saying that "one side loves to drink, the other side hates to pee." But on Sundays in port it was borderline mandatory to attend the services of the Church of England, especially so when the ship's chaplain organized the function. So Higgs was dragged along.

Their first conversation had gone surprisingly well. Although neither attractive nor unattractive—nondescript was the best word for Higgs—he did not stare at her or make any socially unacceptable remarks about her appearance, partly because he was too hung over to be especially observant, but partly because he was an officer in the king's navy and expected to act like a gentleman. Too tired to get drawn too far into her political world, he nevertheless managed to succeed in getting her to think about some of her assumptions without getting cut to pieces.

•   •   •

"Tell me, why is it that men drink so much, Mr. Higgs? It's poison you know."

"Quite right, that. I wish I had had your wise counsel last night," he said, putting the back of his hand to his forehead. "Truth is, maam, that soldiers and sailors have done this since time immemorial—helps one to screw up courage to face the barrel of a gun."

"I suppose," she replied impatiently, stopping to think about this. "But that's another thing, why do men have to fight so much? Isn't world peace infinitely superior to the barbarism of war?"

Higgs did not rebuke her, or mock her, as many men would have done. He merely said, taking an oblique approach: "Quite right again, maam. I agree. You see," he said, pointing to her and then to himself, "great minds *do* work alike. But until we can convince the Kaiser too I'm afraid we Englishmen will have to stand watch."

"Wage war to end war, then? There's something strangely convoluted about that logic don't you think?"

He shrugged and said nothing. She also said nothing for a moment. Finally she said: "Well at least you don't seem to think that a woman's brain is smaller than a man's—how many times have we suffragettes heard that?"

"Tommy rot, that idea, pure rubbish," replied Higgs.

She just looked at him, pleasantly surprised that at least there was one man who was not so seemingly simple and one-dimensional.

• • •

On subsequent summer calls to port, I went to other church socials, had other conversations with Anne Mari, and even got a few invitations to the Haga home. Our friendship—I guess that's what you would call it—grew to include some correspondence during the many months when I was at sea and she finished her studies in Oslo. When *Glasgow* entered the harbor that early October weekend of 1914, therefore, I once again found myself at the Haga family dinner table.

The culinary portion of the evening passed without much more than polite conversation, for it was customary in that day not to politicize dinner conversation—and this was one custom, at least, that the Hagas observed. Once the table was cleared, however, the evening became an unusual mix of the old and the new. We two men repaired to the living room to discuss more serious matters, but mother and daughter, who would typically have been excluded, came along. There were no cigars for us either, and in a sad compromise between our thirst and the temperance sensitivities of the women, only two glasses of the best Norwegian aquavit were served. And then the bottle was locked away in the cabinet.

• • •

The elder Haga asked what was on the mind of everybody in Port Stanley—and what was especially worrisome in shipping circles from the Falklands to Montevideo on the River Platte: "Will those German ships come 'round the Horn to raid commerce, Mr. Higgs?"

Mathilda Haga quickly added her own concern: "Should we evacuate the town? Terrible rumors are filtering back from Europe about the Germans shooting thousands of civilian hostages in Belgium."

Anne Mari remained silent, but she had not heard about the atrocities in Belgium and this clearly startled her. She turned to Higgs, anxious to hear his reply.

"As soon as the squadron has finished coaling most of us have orders to put back to sea to reconnoiter for the Germans off the coast of Chile. The flagship remains here to await reinforcements. So to answer your question, Mrs. Haga, have no fear for the safety of civilians in the Falklands. If the enemy tries to break into the South Atlantic, which is what we all expect, we'll give him a rude welcome."

Anne Mari kept silent, but the prospect of her friend in a titanic clash at sea unsettled her more. She put her hand over her mouth and her eyes widened in alarm.

Seeing that his words had upset Anne Mari, Higgs pondered briefly what to say. Pacifism in the abstract had collided with the stark realities of a world at war—this was evident from the look on her face, which no longer displayed the usual chin-up confidence.

"I've always known it could come to this, Anne Mari. I know you have too. Anyway, we don't know where Admiral Spee's squadron is. He could have turned back—Admiralty thinks so in fact—or perhaps he will try to pass through the Panama Canal and into the Caribbean. There's no reason to be overly alarmed, my friends."

And then, taking a stab at humor, he proclaimed: "How about let's all have a round of aquavit!"

Carl Haga was caught off guard and momentarily did not know what to say, but then smiled in anticipation, as if Higg's ploy might just work. The women both raised fingers in a sign of scolding, but then all, quickly noticing that Higgs had winked, and had clearly just been joking, had a good laugh.

•   •   •

On Monday, October 5th, Higgs came back aboard *Glasgow* and left Port Stanley with *Monmouth* and *Ortanto* for the Straits. Two days later Cradock received a message from Admiralty informing him that Spee was indeed steaming for Easter Island and Chile. He knew that *Canopus*, a slower ship, would take a few more days to reach Port Stanley, but supposedly *Defence* had already left the Mediterranean to join his squadron. A week passed with no reinforcement and, worse for the impatient Cradock, no word. So where was she?

While the captain of *Good Hope*, Peter Francklin, occupied the crew with mundane tasks and an occasional foray into the Atlantic for target practice—which the older reservists and young teenage cadets who had been hurriedly mobilized to man the two older vessels of the squadron in August sorely needed—the admiral had little to do but anxiously observe these drills, read in his cabin, and then when dinner hour approached, go ashore to Government House for a pleasant evening with Allardyce. The sight of Cradock and Nelson hurrying up the street to the governor's stately two-storied stuccoed villa made the residents of town feel good. They felt safer with the British navy there to protect them.

Meanwhile, *Glasgow* and the rest of Cradock's squadron passed through the Straits and patrolled the coast of Chile as far as Valparaiso, searching in vain for some sign of the Germans. Their passage across the Pacific had been set back two weeks by Graf Spee's questionable decision to pounce on Samoa and bombard Papeete, expending time, coal, and a hundred irreplaceable shells in the process. They would not sail from Easter Island until October 18th.

• • •

On Thursday, October 15th, a cold, windy, altogether dreary day, HMS *Glasgow* dropped anchor in the roadstead of the Chilean port of Valparaiso. The British vessel was one of the newer light cruisers in the Royal Navy, faster and heavier-armed than SMS *Dresden*, which she had hunted for the past five weeks. The Union Jack proudly caught every changing direction of the wind from high atop the ship.

This day Britain's ensign flew as a minority of one, however, for fifteen flags bearing the black, white, and red colors of Imperial Germany flapped and fluttered all over the harbor. These were steamers of the Kaiser's merchant marine, having found asylum in a neutral port and avoided being taken as prizes by the enemy. To a man the German sailors on deck when *Glasgow* made her appearance cast angry stares at the lone intruder who now had to take sole responsibility for their involuntary exile from the Fatherland and their having to face the ugly possibility of never seeing Germany again.

Glasgow's steam launch pulled away from the mother ship and headed to shore, passing several provisioning boats that would soon bring aboard supplies. Standing with the helmsman and a security detail, the only passenger of rank, Lieutenant Commander Lloyd Higgs, had dispatches for Admiralty from John Luce. Although *Glasgow*'s skipper had thus far reconnoitered unsuccessfully for *Dresden*, he could report no signs of German steamship activity. This augured well, for the absence of fresh colliers off the coast of Chile meant the East Asiatic Squadron would not arrive any time soon.

• • •

As Higgs stepped off the launch the British naval attaché in Valparaiso waited there to meet him. They walked briskly through the streets toward the consulate. Underway a bookstore window display caught Higg's attention. "We have time, don't we? Let's take a look at this."

They moved up to the storefront to inspect a war map of Europe studded with little colored flags connected with black threads to indicate the opposing battle lines. A clerk finished updating things in the east, where red-flagged German and Austro-Hungarian positions had pushed green-flagged Russian counters back closer to Warsaw. On the western front the same red flags and black threads, confronted by blue and white flags of the French and British, snaked from the

Swiss border to the northeast of Paris and then northwards almost to the English Channel, stopping in western Belgium near a town called Ypres.

"The Germans have bitten off more than they can chew," said Higgs confidently.

"*Could* be," replied his escort with somewhat less assurance.

As they conversed, both noticed a young, smartly dressed man who also looked at the map. The Englishmen did not think he had heard or understood what they said, but suddenly, jerking his head away from the display like a hunter about to trap his prey, the gamesman cast what can only be described as an angry smile at them. Speechless and a little taken aback, the two went along their way.

"I must say," exclaimed Higgs, "this is an extraordinary town. "Here we are in uniform, and no one has as much as spoken a word to us. Did you see that chap at the window? He looked at me, an officer of the Royal Navy, as if I were some wild beast!"

"This *is* an extraordinary town," said the other man. "It's full of German émigrés who hate us, want Germany to win the war and rule the world, and can't understand or tolerate why Chile is still neutral."

They walked on.

• • •

The man in question looked contemptuously at his foes as they disappeared around the corner. After a moment he turned back to study the map for a few more minutes before stepping inside the door to Reinhardt's Bookstore and Café. He moved left past customers perusing the shelves and into the café area, taking a seat with a young woman who had been waiting, a little impatiently, for a few minutes.

"I see my beautiful, black-eyed fiancée is ready for her mid-day meal," he said, leaning down to kiss her cheek.

"Flattery will get you nowhere, Hansi," she said jokingly. "Germans are usually more punctual," she went on only a little more seriously. The young woman's illuminated smile gave visual testimony to her deep inner happiness.

"Guilty as charged. And, well, sorry. I know it's less important than being on time, but I wanted to see if our armies have taken Paris and Warsaw."

"So *sarcastic* are we today ... Is everything all right with you?"

• • •

Johannes Bauer had just turned thirty-three years old in October 1914. He hailed from Kiel, naval base of the German Baltic Fleet, where at seventeen years of age he had volunteered, served the regular naval tour of three years, and reenlisted for five. By 1906 Bauer had risen to the rank of petty officer with the torpedo crews of the older cruisers and pre-dreadnought battleships that patrolled the Baltic Sea. Faced with the choice of advancing to be a non-commissioned "deck officer," or leaving the service, he chose the latter, for he had seen enough of the denigrating way regular officers treated deck officers to know that he would not be respected.

Bauer went instead to Chile at the behest of his great uncle, Heinrich Hermann Bauer. Forced to flee Germany after participating in the revolutions of 1848-1849, the twenty-year old had migrated to Chile. He joined other compatriots there who farmed land that was more plentiful, and easier to buy, than in the over-populated countryside of Germany. He had no success at relationships and never married, but success in agriculture led over the decades to success as a grain trader, and eventually he accumulated enough capital to open a successful bank in Valparaiso.

The decades passed and his career seemed close to an end, but then the great earthquake of August 1906 interrupted. This curse from nature—8.2 on the Richter scale—killed thousands of people in the inner-harbor. Fires raged for days, killing many thousands more. Some estimates placed the death toll at 20,000. The Chilean government poured millions into disaster relief and reconstruction, and a portion of this aid was filtered through Bauer's bank. He was already seventy-eight years old, however, and although still robust, longed for a younger man to carry some of the workload. Hence the invitation to his grand nephew, Johannes, who talked it over with his parents, resigned from the navy, and sailed for South America.

The old man groomed the younger one in the ins and outs of banking as the years drew on to 1914 and the city sprang back to life. By this time Johannes essentially ran the bank and Heinrich Hermann Bauer limited himself to one weekly advisory meeting.

Over these years the senior man had also provided entrée to the upper tier of German émigré soci-
ety, including one of the most important Germans in
Valparaiso, Vice-Counsel Heinrich von Eichhorn, and
thereby a chance to meet arguably the most beautiful young lady in town, the diplomat's twenty-three
year old daughter, Simone, whose "black-eyed"
good looks she got from her deceased Chilean
mother, not the mousey-looking Eichhorn. Johannes
and Simone became engaged in the spring of 1914
and were planning to be married in June 1915. But
on this late winter day in 1914 war was beginning to
crowd thoughts of domestic bliss out of the young
man's mind.

• • •

"Well of course I don't think I made a mistake by
leaving the navy—otherwise I wouldn't have met you—
but ..."

Simone cut him off softly. "But? This sounds ominous."

Johannes looked at her, still patient, but with an
expression that asked, even pleaded, for her to be a
tolerant listener while he explained himself. He knew
she would.

"Let me try it another way. You remember this spring
when Prince and Princess Heinrich visited aboard the
new battleships *Kaiser* and *König Albert*. Well, after the
parade of their sailors I went aboard and spoke to some
of the deck officers on the torpedo crews. They openly
grumbled about their lowly social status, having different uniforms than the regulars, not being allowed to

have mess with the "real" officers, and so on. That confirmed for me the wisdom of leaving and coming here. But five months later those same deck officers were at war, ready to give their lives for the Fatherland. They were ready for a man's rite of passage, but I was not. It made me feel kind of cowardly and boyish. I think that's why I study these maps outside so zealously. I want the war to end soon in a German victory, and then I will be able to feel better about myself, to feel normal again. Does this make sense?"

Simone smiled lovingly and said nothing for a moment. Then she leaned over the table and kissed Johannes. "Whether you fight or don't fight you're a good man, Hansi."

Her fiancée looked at her as if to say: "How can you be so sure?"

Seeing this, Simone changed tack a bit. "Look, I too want Germany to win the war quickly, and I think Germany will prevail. God will punish England. But I have to confess to selfish motives. Chile is neutral. The war will not come here, which means my man will stay safe and sound. Our future together stays safe and sound. We will have children, and grandchildren. Have you seen how Uncle Heinrich looks at you, how proud of you he is? I want that kind of look for us. So let God punish England so you don't have to. I want God to hold his hand over your head."

Now Johannes smiled. He placed his hand over hers. "I love you Simone."

"Too," she said.

· · ·

Later that day, having finished his business ashore, Higgs returned to his ship. Fully provisioned, *Glasgow* weighed anchor and steamed back to the south.

•   •   •

While still waiting and worrying in the Falklands the same day, October 15th, Cradock received doubly negative, especially disappointing news. First, *Canopus* had more engine troubles in Montevideo. Second, *Defence* would not join his command after all, but rather form the core of a second squadron based off the River Platte, commanded by Rear Admiral A. P. Stoddart. The big armored cruiser represented a second line of defense in case Spee eluded Cradock's flotilla and suddenly appeared off Argentina to wreck havoc on British shipping. To Cradock, reading pessimistically between the lines of Admiralty's message, "eludes your flotilla" could also mean "destroys your flotilla." Was he, then, so expendable? Did he have enemies in London, maybe Mountbatten and Sturdee, who conspired against him?

•   •   •

On Sunday the 18th the Hagas went to church while Anne Mari, not feeling particularly well, stayed home to read the—to her—scandalous anti-feminist tract of Otto Weininger, *Gender and Character*. The weather was also not especially inviting—mid-October in the Falklands brings much snow. Her parents entered the living room and sat down, both looking worried. Mathilda Steen had obviously been crying.

"Is anything wrong, Mama?" Then, before any reply, she turned to her father. "Papa?"

"Nothing's the matter, my dear. It's just that the service was so moving, so poignant, so ... " He paused to find words to do justice to what he felt.

"Poignant indeed," said Mathilda, wiping the last tears from her cheeks. "*Good Hope*'s padre, the Reverend Arthur Pitt, came ashore with what seemed like half the ship's company to preach at the cathedral. It was packed—Governor Allardyce, Admiral Cradock, Captain Francklin, so many of the officers, midshipmen, and the cadets in their Eton jackets and gold buttons. They looked such children. His sermon was so very touching. I was not the only one who wept: '... and after all it was Christ who made the supreme sacrifice so that we who came after might be saved. The time may be not far distant when we may be called upon to do the same, and who are we to flinch from following our Lord's example and laying down our lives so that our folks at home shall be saved from the domination of a ruthless foe.'"[6]

As Mathilda recited the chaplain's words, she seemed to enter another trance-like dimension, almost as if in a séance. The sight of this gave Anne Mari a chilling feeling. She pulled her shawl more tightly around her shoulders. "Papa, if the Germans get through, will you join the other men in the militia?"

"I already have, my dear."

---

6   From Hickling, *Sailor at Sea*. See my methodological Afterword.

The Haga family sat in silence. No one said anything because there was nothing more to say. The need to defend hearth and home if necessary was so real, while the lofty goal of the peace movement, a world without war, seemed abstract to the point of irrelevance. The message of Christ's Sermon on the Mount, love thy enemy, seemed now equally irrelevant—the good Reverend Pitt had completely suppressed it.

• • •

At noon on October 22nd Cradock and Nelson once again ambled up the way to Governor's House. It was not suppertime, thus the unexpected appearance of his friend surprised Allardyce. Noticing Cradock's troubled demeanor, the governor left his work desk and escorted him into a sitting room where they could talk alone. The Royal Navy's guardian of the islands sat down, said nothing, and just shook his head.

Allardyce lit a pipe and cast a worried glance at the admiral. "Why the long face, Kit? Everyone on the island saw mighty *Canopus* steam into the harbor this morning. Surely the arrival of her big guns after so much delay is good news indeed?"

But there was no reply, only a sort of disapproving growl. Nelson felt his master's anger and moved paws over snout coweringly. "Kit, whatever is the matter?" pleaded Allardyce, obviously even more concerned.

Finally the old salt mustered himself. "It's bad enough that Admiralty has denied me *Defence*—this you know—but *Canopus* is a white elephant. Her guns are big, but their range is short, and they're manned by reservists, while Spee's gun layers are the best in Germany. And today the elephant's captain informed me that the old reciprocating steam engines are broken down—without extensive repairs she'll only make twelve knots—twelve knots against Spee's twenty-two?! *Canopus* stays here until she can make better speed."

This startled Allardyce. Although frightened for Cradock, he thought it wise to say nothing and let the man continue. His friend obviously had more to say.

"I sail for the Straits this afternoon, Allardyce. There are two things I want you to do for me, if you would be so kind?"

"Certainly, if I can. What is it?"

"I shall not see you again. In this box are my medals and decorations. If the Germans do come here and occupy these islands please bury them. Then when the war is over I would be grateful if you would send them to my people. Here is my address." He handed over the box and a piece of paper with his address in England.

"Of course, of course," said Allardyce, looking quite distraught. "What else?"

"I have a letter here for Admiral Hedworth Meux, an old friend of mine. Post this in the event that my squadron completely disappears—and me with it. This letter is my defense against the treatment meted out to me from London. I have no intention, after forty years at sea, of being an unheard victim!"

Saying this, Cradock rose from his chair, handed the letter to Allardyce, extended his hand, and said "farewell." He motioned, and Nelson followed him obediently to the door.

Nearly dumbfounded by now, Allardyce only barely managed to say "Godspeed."

• • •

That grey and blustery afternoon *Good Hope* rounded the lighthouse, her four large funnels making huge clouds of smoke, and disappeared from view. Many of the young women who knew the sailors stood on the stone jetty waving goodbye with what must have been half of the town. The flagship's smoke lingered longer than the ship, mixing and eventually merging with angry dark clouds, an occasional ray of sunlight shining into this ominous kaleidoscope in the sky. Soon this too disappeared and the Kelpers drifted away to their homes. It was known that *Canopus* would be leaving in a few days. They would be left to their own devices. Hearts were as heavy as the weather in Port Stanley.

XIV
OFF CORONEL

By October 27th Cradock had reached the Vallenar Islands, just off the coast of Chile about 650 miles south of Valparaiso. Here he joined the remainder of his squadron and took on coal. Lieutenant Commander Higgs left *Glasgow* for *Monmouth* and *Good Hope* to collect outgoing mail. His cruiser was to be detached that evening for Coronel, 350 miles farther up the coast, to deliver mail and pick up the latest dispatches from Admiralty relayed over the telegraph line from Montevideo.

Higgs went first to the wardroom of *Monmouth*, where he awaited the officers of the various divisions who brought letters home from their sailors. The mood was tense: all considered action against Spee in the next few days inevitable, but did not like the odds. One lieutenant commander who had known Higgs for years took him aside to hand over a farewell message. "See that this gets to my wife, Lloyd. I've got a terrible feeling about what lurks out there in the soup. *Glasgow* has got speed, so she can get away, but we are for it, old chap."

Higgs knew what role he had to play. "Come now, we'll all muddle through. Drinks on me in the "Rose and

Crown." There were no airs or high-hatting with Uncle Lloyd. He gathered up his mail bags and departed for the flagship.

On board *Good Hope* Higgs braced himself for encountering the same bleak outlook, which he did while waiting in the wardroom. He grew more and more uncomfortable listening to men of the Royal Navy make gloomy remarks. And then something dreadful came over him and into him, making his skin crawl. It was as if some alien presence forced Higgs to sense the horror stalking Cradock's squadron. He stood up to shake off this frighteningly creepy feeling, but a messenger announced that the admiral wanted to see him.

Higgs entered the head man's Spartan cabin and snapped to attention: "Lieutenant Commander Higgs reporting as ordered sir." Cradock told him to stand easy.

"If we get into a scrap, which is why we're here, Higgs, I want a man with your expertise on the flagship. Gather your things and transfer to *Good Hope*."

"Yes sir," said Higgs, and then started to say something, but hesitated.

"What is it Higgs?"

"Sir, let me respectfully suggest that I stay with *Glasgow* until we return from Coronel. There will be dispatches from Admiralty to decode."

"Agreed." Seeing that there was still something on Higg's mind, Cradock barked: "Spit it out Higgs!" The admiral was clearly out of sorts, and had been since leaving Port Stanley.

SOUTH AMERICA
(Peter Groesbeck)

As for the junior man, the fatalistic mood he had seen on both ships had unnerved him—and Cradock's angry demeanor only added to this uneasiness. "Sir, by your leave, I'd like to report to Captain Luce about the prospects for squadron receiving reinforcements."

Cradock looked ready to explode. He stared at Higgs threateningly. Finally he blurted out: "Yes, Luce needs to know. *Canopus* steams toward us, two days away, but she won't be of much use to us in finding and destroying the enemy until she makes better speed. So yesterday I ordered Admiral Stoddart in Montevideo to detach *Defence*. If Admiralty backs me up, she too will be with us soon. So don't be the messenger bearing bad news from Coronel, Higgs! Carry on."

Glasgow raised steam and left Vallenar for Coronel a few hours later.

• • •

Already nearing her destination on October 29th, *Glasgow* reported hearing heavy wireless traffic—"Le, Le, Le"—in the vicinity. Judging from the strength of the signals, the sender was perhaps only 300 miles away. The messages used the call sign of one of Spee's light cruisers, SMS *Leipzig*. After reading this dispatch from *Glasgow*, Cradock signaled his ramshackle flotilla to raise steam and head north in order to catch this lone prey.

They had been at sea for only an hour when *Canopus* steamed slowly into the islands—on schedule, but, not surprisingly, reporting more engine problems. His mood worsening, Cradock wired the battleship and ordered her captain to make the necessary repairs and hurry north to join the rest of the squadron—in time, he hoped, for a showdown with the rest of Spee's ships. If *Defence* had left Montevideo three days earlier, as Cradock hoped, then she too would soon enter Chilean waters.

. . .

In London, meanwhile, Churchill had been rather preoccupied with a major staff change in the Admiralty: Lord Mountbatten had stepped down and Churchill awaited the new First Sea Lord, none other than the father of Britain's dreadnought and battle cruiser revolution, John "Jacky" Fisher, who would begin work October 30th.

Cradock's last wireless before reaching Vallenar, however, had irked the First Lord. Was the headstrong Cradock countermanding Admiralty's decision to assemble two strong squadron's to snare Graf Spee, one on the east coast with *Defence* at its core, one on the west with the citadel-like *Canopus*? So Churchill fired off a reply to Cradock on October 28th: "*Defence* is to remain on east coast under orders of Stoddart. This will leave sufficient force on each side in case hostile cruisers appear there on the trade route."

On the 30th Churchill briefed Fisher on the deployment of Royal Navy ships throughout the world, including the Eastern Pacific/South Atlantic, which he described as "the critical point." Afterwards, turning to the new First Sea Lord, he said: "You don't suppose Cradock would try to fight them without *Canopus*?"

Fisher, who as a navy man clearly had a lesser opinion of the old ship than the politician over him, did not know what to say.

•   •   •

We completed the eight-day voyage from Easter Island to Más Afuera on October 26th. The East Asiatic anchored beneath a volcanic cliff that rose sharply 3,000 feet above the sea. Our crews repeated the blackening business of feeding the ships. The squadron spent several melancholy days in the shelter of this gigantic rock, which frowned upon the Pigmy vessels below and bore silent, sinister witness to our labor. The huge stone face mocked us, eerily seeming to know that we sailed somewhere into oblivion.[7]

On October 28th, during a bright moonlit night, we quitted the ugly rock. Its massive outline remained long in view. During the next night we glimpsed the far-off lights of Valparaiso. And then on October 30th, in glorious sunlight still out at sea, we saw the snow-capped summit of Aconcagua, the highest mountain of South America, rising above the peaks of the Cordilleras beyond the haze of the coast of Chile. Our first objective—crossing the wide Pacific—was attained.

All hands, nearly 3,000 of us, felt pressure building up in our "mines" about what would happen next. The enemy came from the south—this we knew already

---

7   From Pochhammer, *Before Jutland*. See my methodological Afterword.

for weeks, indeed exactly which ships. England came to dispute the mastery of the sea on this very coast. To make sure of an encounter, we knew our admiral would not question confronting that enemy. This was Graf Spee's destiny—even if, as seemed certain, the foe had sent a battleship to stop us, our admiral would confront them.

On Saturday, October 31st, after the colliers had signaled that they had all reached neutral ports in Chile, we turned south, keeping at a great distance from the land to avoid detection.

• • •

During the night watch Graf Spee rested in his cabin, dozing lightly. He had been pondering the complex logistics of rendezvousing with colliers that were positioned in ports all along the south-central coast of Chile. Someone knocked. He opened the door. "Yes, Fielitz, what is it?"

"Sir, one of our colliers has wired that a British light cruiser, the *Glasgow*, has anchored in Coronel."

"Bring the captain and first officer to the conference room in ten minutes."

Once the brain trust of the squadron had assembled, Spee announced his plan. "Gentlemen, all ships have been signaling for days with the call sign of *Leipzig*. If the *Glasgow* has swallowed this hook and believes she can catch a scouting light cruiser, clearly weaker than her, all alone, we can descend on Coronel, and destroy the only modern vessel they have."

Spee then unfolded a chart of the approach channels to Coronel. "*Nürnberg* will first ascertain whether *Glasgow* is still there. If so, *Gneisenau* and *Leipzig* will skirt south of Santa Maria Island and enter the bay off Coronel, *Scharnhorst* and *Dresden* will enter the bay from the northeast side of the island. How do you view the situation?"

The plan seemed sound enough and there was no discussion. "All right then, signal the rest of the squadron with Morse lamps."

As the others filed out, Spee motioned Fielitz back. "Have the communications officer report to me."

Minutes later the man appeared. "Schmidt, is there news from our agents in Chile about *Emden*?"

"Nothing much, sir. She appears to have attempted a raid on the English at Penang, Malaysia, but we don't know the outcome."

Spee nodded pensively, but said nothing, obviously wondering if four hundred of his sailors still lived.

"Is that all sir?"

"Yes Schmidt, carry on."

• • •

We dropped anchor in Coronel at 1830 hours on October 31st.[8] The British consul came aboard, bringing news, mostly bad, of the European fighting on land and sea. Our army was still stuck in the trenches of France. The navy's blockade of Germany held tight, but some of our older heavy cruisers had been torpedoed in the Channel with great loss of life and one of

8   From Hirst, *Coronel and After*. See my methodological Afterword.

the newer dreadnought battleships had struck a mine and sunk, improving the odds a bit for Germany.

The consul also emphasized the completeness of the German intelligence network in Chile, which was confirmed by a wireless message we intercepted at 0200, November 1st, informing Von Spee of our presence in the harbor. A German merchant ship in Coronel had probably sent the wireless. This made Captain Luce sense danger—he decided to leave as early as possible.

The remainder of the night we dispatched the mails and telegrams and decoded telegrams awaiting Admiral Cradock. As we did this, more strong wireless messages came through, removing from our minds any vestiges of doubt that a German light cruiser reconnoitered the area. Glasgow weighed anchor at 0900 and steamed north to fool German intelligence, and then back to the southwest at 20 knots through increasingly choppy seas. We rendezvoused with Cradock's ships at 1300.

A very heavy sea was running by this time with a strong southerly wind, making the lowering of boats impossible. Consequently the messages we brought were transferred to Good Hope by placing them in a six-inch gun cartridge case and towing the case across the flagship's bow. They fished it out of the water and brought it aboard. Because of the worsening storm I could not transfer my billet to Good Hope. It was with no small sense of relief that I stayed on Glasgow. At least this was how I felt at the time, a feeling that would later brand my soul with guilt and shame.

•   •   •

When *Glasgow* performed her maneuver with the cartridge case Cradock stood on the bridge with Francklin, and then went below to read the dispatches. Churchill's telegram brought a scowl to its reader's face, but it did not surprise him after the developments of the last three weeks. The admiral walked back to the bridge, mumbling angrily and sarcastically about the "sufficient force" Admiralty had bequeathed him. He knew this would likely be a deadly legacy, but he had duty to do.

Once fore Cradock issued orders for the squadron to fan out into a sweeping column fifteen miles abreast to seek and destroy *Leipzig*, which he believed lay somewhere to the north reconnoitering ahead of the East Asiatic. On the left flank, farthest out to sea, came *Good Hope*, then *Monmouth*, then *Ortanto*, with *Glasgow* on the right some fifty miles from shore.

They cruised for a little over two hours at 12 knots, *Glasgow* moving a little faster and pulling a few miles ahead of the north-northeasterly sweep. With the seas getting rougher still at 1620 hours, her masthead lookout hailed out: "Smoke, bearing green four-five!" Luce, First Officer Wilfred Thompson, and others on the bridge immediately swung their glasses to four points off the starboard bow. "It's probably the *Orcoma*, Chilean merchantman due in Coronel this evening," speculated the captain.

Minutes later, however, as *Glasgow* picked up speed and altered course eastwards to investigate, a signalman with telescope to his eye called out: "Two warships with four funnels, one warship with three—no, two warships with three funnels—four warships bearing green five-o!" Luce, studying what was coming into focus, quickly drew his conclusions: "It's *Scharnhorst*, *Gneisenau*, and the whole bloody East Asiatic Squadron. There will be the devil to pay. Turn about and fall back on the flagship. Signal 'Enemy-in-Sight.' Sound general quarters."

The British had indeed spotted the East Asiatic, minus *Nürnberg*, which had fallen back to stop a merchant ship. *Gneisenau* led the line, followed by *Leipzig*, *Dresden*, and *Scharnhorst*, the order of battle Spee had issued for the descent into Coronel. The moment *Glasgow* had seen smoke, *Leipzig* had too. She immediately veered out of line to investigate. After a few minutes she signaled the squadron: "Enemy light cruiser in sight."

The German ships sounded battle stations and changed course four points to starboard. As they steamed west-southwest *Scharnhorst*, with more boilers in action, overtook the others and raced to the head of the line, *Gneisenau* now second.

• • •

The drum rattled the order: "Clear the decks for action." Throughout the ship came the tension-breaking cry: "The English are yonder." It seemed as if all our cares, inside and out, had vanished. The men flew, light as birds, just as they had drilled many times, up and down stairs, across the decks, wherever their special duties took them. Ship's boats were hoisted and fastened to their cleats. The gun crews flew at their work, ramming charges in: our gunners, like ancient Etruscan warriors, crouched at their battle stations with smiles on their faces. The fires of the boilers burned like the fires of hell on the Day of Judgment. It was Sunday, November 1st: All Saint's Day for us.[9]

• • •

On *Glasgow* Thompson had finished his inspection round of the ship by 1700. He reported on the bridge that all stations were ready for action. "You know, Number One," Luce said to him, "in my opinion I think we might be able to rendezvous with *Canopus* by dawn tomorrow. She's finally away from Vallenar, heading our way. But, knowing the admiral as I do, I expect he will fight. He is constitutionally incapable of refusing or even postponing action if there is the smallest chance of success."

Luce did in fact know Cradock well, for just minutes later he ordered the squadron to concentrate on *Glasgow*'s position. Higgs received the message and passed along its contents through his speaking tube. Rather than flee west and south into the darkness that was only hours away, rather than fall back on his citadel, the hard-charging Cradock went east instead, formed into line, and turned south on a parallel course

---

9   From Pochhammer, *Before Jutland*. See my methodological Afterword.

with the Germans—*Good Hope* in the van, followed by *Monmouth*, *Ortanto*, and *Glasgow*.

At 1804 they all turned four points to port in order to close the distance and get into range for the squadron's 6-inch guns. Only *Good Hope* had anything heavier—two 9.2-rifles. At 1818 Cradock radioed *Canopus*, some 250 miles to the south: "I am now going to attack the enemy."

By this time Spee had formed his battle line, too, about ten miles away. On his bridge over the past hour the German nobleman had gone from one surprise to another. They were mostly pleasant surprises. "It's not the *Glasgow* alone," he said to Schultz at 1720, "but the whole British squadron."

"They'll get a drubbing all the same," replied the captain of the German flagship. "And look," Schultz continued, "the third ship in line is not a queen-class battleship—they have none—it's a converted liner." This observation relieved much of the anxiety in both men, for action would be accepted, come what may.

They continued to peer through their glasses at the British ships. At 1747 *Good Hope*'s top flags were discernable. "Good Lord," exclaimed Spee, "it *is* Kit Cradock."

He lowered his binoculars, turned to Schultz, and shook his head sadly. "My old friend is in the wrong place at the wrong time. It would be better for him if he got out of my way. I should be sorry to have to sink him."

And when Cradock changed course, Spee ordered: "Hard to port. I'm not ready for him yet with the setting sun in our eyes. In an hour, with the sun down nicely and silhouetting his whole line, only then will we commence fire."

They both left the bridge for the armored conning tower, directly below them, and peered out through the slits of their castle.

•   •   •

When the sun was sufficiently low on the horizon as not to blind our gunnery officers, and the English ships were sharply outlined against the blaze of the setting sun, while the lofty Chilean coast, dark and cloud-capped, formed our background and obscured us from view, the East Asiatic Squadron, on a signal from *Scharnhorst* at 1820 hours, moved a point towards the enemy.[10] This was the attack maneuver, and the order ran through the ship: "Prepare for long distance firing by starboard batteries."

The minutes passed, full of suspense; 1830 hours, 1840 hours, 1850 hours ... The range narrowed: 15,000 yards, 14,000 yards, 13,000 yards ... Although every man was at his station, thoughts turned to the impending battle, or alighted for a moment on the homeland. What would our comrades say, and our friends and families, who may have long given us up for lost? We were going to show them that we were still alive, that in spite of our long distance from home we were

---

10   From Pochhammer, *Before Jutland*. See my methodological After-word.

fighting with them on the same common front against England.

And then, at exactly 1904 hours, a thunderclap ripped across the water and brought us back to the deadly business at hand. In my armored central station the helmsman's mate listening at the speaking tube cried out: "*Scharnhorst* has opened fire on *Good Hope*!" Almost at the same moment we fired our first shots at *Monmouth*. Our whole ship trembled. Now our heavy cruisers were firing one broadside after another. Every twenty seconds, then every fifteen, all starboard guns roared their steely battle music into the stormy evening air.

• • •

In their armored tower Cradock, flanked by Francklin and the chief gunnery officer, saw the muzzle flashes from *Scharnhorst*'s broadside: six 8.2-inch guns. A few seconds later came the deafening crack of sound. The range was still long—12,500 yards—and the salvo fell 500 yards to the port side. "500 short," said the gunnery officer confidently.

The British commanders stood there, poised and calm. Pre-battle fears had yielded right of way to professional preoccupation with duty. This was the Royal Navy, after all, and soon, despite a stormy sea and a nearly totally obscured German target camouflaged by the dark shore at dusk, two bigger guns would return fire and tear into the metal of Spee's flagship. Francklin ordered: "Fore and aft mounts train on the flash and stand by to open fire."

Seconds later they saw more muzzle flashes and then heard the booming sound of another salvo. "500 over," the man reported—with alarm, only a trace of confidence left from a moment earlier, for the Germans with frightening efficiency seemed set to zero in on their target despite the distance and intensifying gale. Was this as easy as target practice for them? Would the next shots bring what by now seemed inevitable?

Once again: flashes, then sound, and then shells obliterated the forward gun turret, killing its entire crew instantly, sending flames up to the forecastle, knocking Cradock and his comrades down. Other shells crashed amidships and aft. The flagship burned and yet had not fired a shot. The crack German gunners had gotten three broadsides away while the rusty reservists of *Good Hope* fumbled to get ready.

Francklin's sole remaining gun able to fire at this range finally answered, but the shell sailed wildly over the barely visible *Scharnhorst*. And before it could discharge a second shot two more salvos slammed into the doomed British vessel, blowing away huge chunks of its superstructure, knocking over funnels, and violently transforming other stations above deck into a mess of entangled metal wreckage. All about lay the bloody remains and severed limbs of what minutes earlier had been smartly-uniformed men—and boys in Eton jackets.

Good Hope's aft cannon got off a second shot, which also missed badly, and then with the precision that comes from practice, two more German salvos found their marks. It was 1923. Cradock ordered two points to port in order to close the range for his smaller guns. He also told the radio room to wire his lumbering battleship: "*Canopus* help yourself," but the enemy jammed the signal, such that, in a tragic and ironic twist, only "*Canopus* help" went into the airwaves.

• • •

Meanwhile *Gneisenau* had been pounding *Monmouth*, mercilessly meting out macabre metallic misfortune with every salvo. From the door of his radio room on *Glasgow*, Lloyd Higgs stared in shock at the seemingly cold-blooded execution of squadron comrades who only hours earlier had known in their hearts that "they were for it."

• • •

The scene ahead absorbed the attention of those of us not actively engaged in directing our fire.[11] My heart sank. The Germans broadsides had scored one direct hit after another, such that soon there was a continuous sheet of flame along the length of both *Good Hope* and *Monmouth*, flames so strong that the heavy sea had no dampening effect. Both had difficulty keeping station in the running sea. They were constantly yawing out of line. Frequently our two cruisers flashed into a vivid orange as high explosive shells detonated against

11   From Hirst, *Coronel and After*. See my methodological Afterword.

their upper works. The whole scene was appalling. This was not supposed to happen to the Royal Navy.

We were now under the concentrated fire of *Leipzig* and *Dresden*, their shells falling a few yards short and a few yards over, close enough for the spray to drench our gun crews. Then I felt a shell hit—it was as if some gigantic behemoth two decks below me had given the ship's side a good kick.

• • •

At 1940 hours Cradock ordered another turn to port and charged straight for the enemy, keeping up a desultory fire but hoping to close within range of torpedoes. Spee saw this and did not give his old friend's slower ship the chance—he also turned to port.

And then at 1950 the inevitable happened. One of the countless German shells that continued to pummel *Good Hope* exploded the magazine between the forward funnel and conning tower, sending a column of fire and a ton of debris 200 feet skyward. As the last light of evening disappeared from the sky *Good Hope*'s death throe lit up the windy, icy ocean like a massive fireworks display even more powerful than what nature was dishing out. After it all crashed down, the entire bow quarter, including what was left of the forecastle, broke off and slipped beneath the waves, as if begging for the rest, mercifully, to follow. Cradock, his dog Nelson, and 800 hands—all save none—were dead.

Monmouth was taking on water too, so much fore that her captain attempted to turn about and place stern to sea. Steering a northeasterly course now, she, like *Good Hope* before her, headed toward the Germans, who could now concentrate the fire of all four cruisers. Presently *Monmouth* stopped dead in the water, most of her 800 crewmen dead too, but although listing to port and down by the bows the old ship refused to sink. Spee ordered his squadron hard to starboard in a charge of sorts to finish off the British.

Glasgow swung slowly around the stricken ship from the east. Luce encouraged her to alter course to the northwest and try to save herself. The signal-man flashed this, and then called out the reply as Luce looked on: "I am badly holed. Must keep stern to sea."

It would be *Monmouth*'s last signal. The Germans were bearing down and firing ranging shots. *Glasgow* was not yet hit badly, but all who had observed the precision of the East Asiatic knew that even in the darkness they would soon find the mark.

In the conning tower, Thompson joined Luce. "I cannot leave my admiral," said the captain. "We will attack with torpedoes."

Thompson coolly took out his cigarette case, opened it, and tapped one four or five times on the case to pack it down, as was his habit. Finally he spoke. "Well, sir," said Thompson with an annoying air of superiority, "our moldering Mark III torpedoes have never run straight once this commission." He lit up. "Besides, there is no admiral to leave. What's more, it not only means the loss of another ship and four hundred men, but there'll be no one to tell the tale. *Canopus* will walk straight into them."

Luce hesitated, his anger quickly turning to resignation. "Tell *Monmouth* to make off as best she can. Hard a'starboard. Full ahead together. Portman, steady her on west."

Glasgow quickly reached her top speed of 28 knots and left the East Asiatic behind. Luce gathered up *Ortanto*, which had bolted the line after the first salvo from the German light cruisers straddled her. They headed west, observing in the eastern darkness seventy-five flashes of gunfire—*Nürnberg*, which had finally caught up with the rest of the squadron, was delivering the coup de grace to *Monmouth*. Then the English refugees turned south into the storm. *Glasgow* finally got a wireless through to *Canopus* once she had distanced herself from the German jamming signals. Taking separate routes for now, the three surviving ships of Cradock's squadron began their sorrowful trek back to Port Stanley.

Chruchill and Fisher: "The Almighty created greyhounds to catch hares"
(Press Association)

•   •   •

The Battle of Cornel was over—mercifully, tragically over. Not until November 4th, however, did Churchill and Fisher learn this. The day before they received a message from the British consul in Valparaiso that the *Nürnberg* had been spotted stopping a merchant ship on November 1st with what looked like the rest of the squadron ten miles southwest of her and out to sea. Because London knew now that Spee had not eluded Cradock and slipped around the Horn, and that for the time being the German represented no threat to the east coast of South America, Stoddart was ordered to dispatch HMS *Defence* with all haste to the west coast. The verdict of history—and the overwhelming majority of opinion in the Royal Navy at the time—must be that the Battle of Coronel might have taken a different turn had this decision been made a month earlier.

Cradock, on the other hand, cannot escape his larger share of historical responsibility for the disaster. Even with *Defence* he would have been marginally outgunned in the long-range phase of the battle—and the East Asiatic was superior in gunnery—which is why Churchill argued consistently even two decades later that his headstrong admiral should not have left *Canopus* behind.

Writing to the Countess the day after the battle, an ever-pessimistic Spee confirmed the wisdom of the British First Lord: "The English have another ship hereabouts, a battleship carrying 12-inch guns. Against her we can hardly do anything. Had they kept their force together we should probably have got the worst of it."

XV
VALPARAISO

On the evening of November 2nd Graf Spee, having celebrated his squadron's remarkable victory, went to his cabin, took out pen and stationary, and wrote again to Margarete.

> *"Pacific Ocean, near Valparaiso   November 2nd 1914*
> *The storm and the fury of battle have passed. On a beautiful, sun-kissed day my flagship, accompanied by Gneisenau, passed the light cruisers in review. From the bridge I saw Otto and Heinrich, both of them our pride and joy, cheering with the other assembled crews. At my signal, flags went up with the message: 'With God's help, a glorious victory. Congratulations!' You can hardly imagine the joy which reigns among us. We have at least contributed something to the glory of German arms—although it might not mean much on the whole in view of the enormous number of English ships."*

That Graf Spee had mentioned the big guns of a British battleship and the English preponderance in numbers reflected his actual mood better than the reference to joy running through the squadron. But, true to his nature, he wanted *Graefin* Margarete to brace herself for his martyrdom to the Fatherland. Would it not have been more sensitive, however, more respect-ful of her fear for the welfare of Family Von Spee, to write nothing about the dangers she already knew lurked everywhere in every ocean?

•　•　•

Valparaiso glistened in a cold Chilean sunrise. It was November 3rd. For the jubilant sailors of our East Asiatic Squadron the sight of the shiny town stretch-ing around the bay, the green hills nearby, and more distantly, the gray and white of soaring, snowcapped mountains seemed like a visual reward for the smash-ing victory over the Royal Navy at Coronel. Into the roadstead of the harbor steamed *Nürnberg* flanked by *Gneisenau* and *Scharnhorst*. Respecting international law that dictated only three ships at a time in a neu-tral harbor, and for only twenty-four hours, *Leipzig* and *Dresden* remained offshore.

The harbor brimmed with ships, among them many steamers and tall sailboats flying our homeland's impe-rial colors, refugee vessels which the war and the over-powering fleet of England had driven from the seas. The captain granted restricted permission for their crews and other Germans ashore to visit our ship. Soon our compatriots swarmed aboard.[12]

12　From Pochhammer, *Before Jutland*. See my methodological After-word.

Already when hurrying across the quarterdeck to take my breakfast in the mess room I had been obliged to hold a sort of review of Germans eager to enroll. None had yet heard of Coronel, but as word spread among them their eagerness to enlist knew no bounds. I was surrounded by captains and officers of German ships, navy and army reservists, volunteers and recruits, all showing in their eyes the fear I should not enlist them. When they were all assembled on the middle deck I counted no less than one hundred, which was far more than our chief replacement needs. "I was fighting boatswain on the battleship *Westfalen*." "I used to be on the *Gneisenau*, boatswain's mate, and 8.2-inch casemate." "Captain, you must take me." Such were the words I heard on all sides.

The flagship takes on provisions - and visitors: Too many things to do in a day
(Pochhammer, *Graf Spee's letzte Fahrt*)

"Don't think that things will always go as smoothly as at Coronel—they may turn out quite differently," I told them. "It's all the same to us, captain," said one of them. "We want to go with you." He was very well dressed, earned a good salary in a bank, and had served at Kiel in the 1st Torpedo Division. Like around twenty of the others whose papers I checked, he would not go until I had enlisted him. What patriotism! Where do we find such men?

• • •

Graf Spee's depression was deepening. The premonition of his own death, the death of two sons serving with him, and the destruction of the entire squadron—mass death at sea—weighed down heavily upon his soul. Inside of him survival instincts and family feelings struggled massively with martial callings. The former, in fact, may have been gaining the advantage, but the last thing he wanted was a banquet to honor his "great" victory. He hated such official functions anyway, but, more to the point, this kind of obnoxious public flag waving would only serve to remind his vulnerable fatherly side that a war still raged and duty still called.

• • •

"No, no, Eichhorn, I have too many things to do and only a day to do them," insisted the clearly very tired admiral.

"But sir, Valparaiso is filled with German patriots who speak of nothing else but the glorious victory of your

160

squadron and the amazing successes of the *Emden*. There should be a proper reception … "

Spee cut him off. "What's that you say about the *Emden*? Is there news of her?"

"Why yes, admiral, Captain Müller has become a legend in his own time. Almost every day comes more news of another ship he's captured. British trading circles are apoplectic."

Spee stared at Eichhorn and acknowledged the latest good news, nodding his head arrogantly. Then he came back to the business at hand, his demeanor worsening again. "A reception you say?" He looked at his chief of staff, who gave back a sympathetic "what-could-it hurt" kind of nod. "Well I suppose if I must, I must, but only a modest luncheon at the German Club—and absolutely no speeches!"

•　•　•

Having successfully enlisted aboard *Gneisenau*, Johannes Bauer now faced the more challenging task of announcing and explaining this risky decision to his fiancée. His thoughts raced nervously: "Like every German in town, I've spoken about little else except the war for months. Within minutes, it seemed, every German in town knew that the victorious East Asiatic Squadron had put in to port. Simone is aware of these things too. Perhaps she has sensed, as a woman, what I have done, what I for months have wanted to do? Women sense these things!"

Bauer had talked himself into it. Perhaps explaining himself would not be so difficult. He saw her from a distance on the park bench, one of their favorite places to rendezvous. What would her facial expression reveal? Did she know? He waved, and she waved back.

Johannes sat down next to Simone and looked into her eyes for clues. Calm and relaxed, she eased his anxiety. "When do you ship out?"

"I knew that you would know ... Tomorrow."

"You haven't been yourself for a long time now," she said, resting her head on his shoulder. "The long hands of this war reached out to touch you all the way back in August. Tomorrow those same hands take you away to God knows what—and God knows where. I can only pray for your safe return."

They sat for a long time not saying anything else. Finally, Simone asked: "What time is the luncheon?"

"I should leave now. After Frau Gordeller makes her presentation to the admiral, let's take a long walk, okay?

"Yes, that will be good. All will be good. All will be good."

• • •

At 1130 hours Spee, his heavy cruiser captains Schultz and Maerker, their first officers Bender and Pochhammer, and other officers of the German big ships, all in full dress uniform, took launches to shore where a delegation of Chilean admirals and German dignitaries welcomed them with great pomp. They proceeded at once through the streets. Clearly annoyed, Spee ignored the flashing cameras and the hurrahs of so many resident Germans as he walked with the others to Valparaiso's German Club.

Inside he mounted the grand staircase and strode past portraits of Kaiser William I, Chancellor Otto von Bismarck, Field Marshall Helmuth von Moltke the Elder, the victor over Austria in 1866 and France in 1870, and a large bust of Kaiser Wilhelm the Second. Spee did not ignore these—what German patriot could?—but the whole day was not unfolding according to his orders to Eichhorn.

The head table in the banquet room was reserved for the heroes of the hour and their Chilean naval hosts. The big round tables Germans love so much filled up the rest of the hall, each occupied by German VIPs of Valparaiso and other parts of the country: restaurateurs and all sorts of store owners; heads of the biggest import-export companies; executives of the nitrate mines, who were down from the north; retired officers from the great patriotic victory over the French in 1870, who long ago settled in Germany-friendly Chile and now finally had an opportunity to dust off antiquated, ill-fitting uniforms from the age of the heroes; and of course resident German officialdom, headed up by Eichhorn, who had invited future son-in-law Johannes Bauer as well as the elder Bauer to sit at his table. This was an all-male, testosterone-high gathering.

A platoon of waiters swarmed out of the kitchen, trays laden with every imaginable delicacy, others with bottles of wine tucked under each arm, still others with pitchers of draft beer, two in each hand. One would have thought the Kaiser himself was there, but the contemptuous scorn in Spee's eyes expressed his dim view of the barely tolerable situation better than words.

For fifteen minutes after they had dined Spee and his officers tolerantly drank toasts to their victory offered up to them. Finally one mindlessly inebriated VIP raised his glass and called for all to drink to the "damnation of the British Navy."

Spee stood up erectly, thinking angrily that his old friend Cradock, recently blown to pieces in combat, had just been insulted: "No! I shall only drink to the memory of a gallant and honorable foe!" He downed his glass, threw it down on its side, and marched out of the room. Seeing this, the other officers followed suit, all to the jaw-dropped shock of the civilians—especially at Eichhorn's table—and the Chileans.

Spee and his men walked back through the long corridor, down the staircase, and out of the building. As they did an elderly woman moved out from the crowd that was waiting patiently for the exit of the victorious warriors. Elise Gordeller represented the German Women's Club of Valparaiso, whose members had turned out in great numbers, among them Simone von Eichhorn. The portly matron stepped forward, congratulated Spee on his victory, and offered him a bouquet of flowers.

Several steps behind, Maerker could not quite make out what Spee said to the woman, but the remark certainly startled the dignified well-wisher and her club sisters. Without taking the flowers he went on his way to the harbor.

Catching up as the Count went back down the street, Maerker tried to turn around Spee's macabre, despondent mood. The admiral's old friend usually remained realistic, sometimes even skeptical about the squadron's chances, but like so many of the sailors, waxed very sanguine after the Battle of Coronel.

"We've won an incredible victory, Max. I didn't think it could happen. We've made it this far, and we'll make it home too."

Spee waved him off. "No, no, my friend. I don't like our options—not for a minute. We are quite homeless. We cannot reach Germany. We possess no other secure harbor. We must plough the seas of the world doing as much mischief as we can until our ammunition is exhausted, or a foe far superior in power succeeds in catching us."

The admiral paused, his mood instantly changing to anger. "But I can tell you this," he barked, shaking a fist at Maerker, "when that last day comes those chaps will pay dearly before they take me down!"

Both Maerker and Pochhammer, who stood next to his captain, looked crestfallen by what they had heard. Finally Maerker spoke: "And which seas will we plough next—around Cape Horn to terrorize the trade routes?"

"No, no. Tomorrow we're heading back to Más Afuera. And from there? I don't know anymore."

Now Maerker and Pochhammer, exchanging glances, looked surprised and somewhat incredulous. Back to the west, not immediately on to the south, and then north, and then home? Why the hell not!?

•　•　•

Johannes Bauer exited the German Club and, seeing Simone, went quickly over to her. The young couple walked slowly down the street. Suddenly Johannes stopped and said: "I've got an idea."

"What?"

"What do you say we ride the cable car to the top and take in the view of the harbor?"

"Sure," she replied, her mixed emotions impossible to mask. It was one of those moments in wartime that all who have gone through them have experienced, sometimes more than once. She was happy to be with him, but sad that he was putting to sea the next day. Sadness trumped happiness.

They turned the corner and hurried to the funicular railway station—the coach seemed about ready to leave. Johannes hurriedly bought two tickets. They took seats in front and watched quietly for a moment as the car left the rebuilt town and the white-capped bay farther and farther below them.

Simone broke the silence first, trying to shake her sadness by talking about something else. "Your admiral was kind of rude to Frau Gordeller. Without taking the bouquet he said: 'the flowers will do nicely for my grave.' Imagine that! And then he just walked away. What a strange thing to say and do after winning a great victory and being honored for it by the entire German community of Valparaiso."

"Inside he also acted differently from what I expected," replied Johannes. "One of grandfather's longtime bank officers drank to the damnation of the Royal Navy. The old fellow was admittedly a few sheets to the wind, but these are pretty much the sentiments of all us Germans here. Graf Spee refused to honor this, raising his glass instead to the gallantry of the Englishmen he had just killed. And then he bolted the hall. But I will say: he does strike the fear of God in people. Your father turned white, not so much with anger as with fright. I bet all of Spee's officers and men respect this, well, this *thunder-charisma*. They will follow him anywhere. I will too."

By this time the cable car had reached the summit. As they stepped out, Simone seized on Johannes' last remark to ask the obvious question: "And where will you follow him to? Where will the squadron sail to?" She paused, and then went on: "How dangerous a situation have you gotten yourself into?"

As they strolled over to a scenic view area, Johannes thought carefully about his answer. They reached a low wall and sat down facing one another. He looked into her eyes, and then down at the roadstead. "There she is, Simone," he said pointing and looking at his ship: "SMS *Gneisenau*."

Johannes knew that he could not pause long for just a view, the ostensible reason for coming, before answering—lest the moment fall apart. So he pushed on quickly, continuing to peer out at the sea. "I expect we will remain in South American waters to raid commerce. The English have nothing afloat in this hemisphere as powerful as the East Asiatic Squadron. After Coronel they will not engage in another suicidal action at sea."

"But Hansi ..."

He cut her off. "Please wait, Simone, let me finish," he said while looking at her and then back at the ships. "Everyone in banking circles assumes that the war will not—cannot—last very long. The international economy, especially international finance, is too intertwined between nations ..."

She interrupted. "But, my dear, don't you think, just maybe, that ..."

Turning back from the harbor view and pulling close to her eyes, the young volunteer cut her off to say what he honestly believed—but it was also something he hoped and thought would comfort his future wife: "I'll come back to you, Simone, *I will*. We will be married next spring, *we will*. Next spring there *will be* peace again in the world. And it will *not* be a peace dictated by Germany's enemies."

Simone von Eichhorn was no feminist, but she had been around men long enough to know that they usually made such remarks without the caution and prudence more common to the fairer sex. Rather than say this, however, or continue to press a point, she simply clasped his hand and gave him a loving supportive look.

Later that afternoon she accompanied him to the harbor and hugged him. Johannes stepped down into the launch with a handful of others who were setting off on their patriotic adventures too. She watched the small vessel pull farther and farther away, wondering, as so many women before her had wondered, and countless others after her would wonder too, whether this was her last sight of him. Bitter sweet sorrow, such parting.

XVI
CHARLEVILLE

The daily routine almost never altered for His Imperial Majesty, Kaiser Wilhelm the Second. An important part of his set piece day came in the form of a portfolio of newspaper clippings carefully prepared to please him. On this day, November 5th 1914, the task had been an easy one for the Chief of the Privy Naval Cabinet, Georg von Müller, who brought a stack of articles about the deeds of Germany's East Asiatic Squadron to the emperor's new residence, Villa Bellaire, outside the French town of Charleville and many miles from the muddy, bloody trenches of the bogged-down Western Front.

If Graf Spee sorely underestimated what he had accomplished thus far, and Karl von Müller knew that *Emden* had much more to do, these hyperbolic newspaper pieces went way too far the other way. His Highness decided then and there to award Graf Spee the Iron Cross, First Class, and no fewer than 300 additional Iron Crosses, Second Class, to the most deserving of the officers and crew. Captain Müller and all 400 of his men received the same First and Second Class honors.

The Kaiser, however, was in no mood to risk sunken ships. Despite an adult life filled with boastful blustering, he had never really been in a combative mood, but recent events had made him even less willing to gamble on victory at sea. On August 28th the British lured a light cruiser squadron into the jaws of their battle cruisers in the Heligoland Bight, blowing three victims to bits, including two modern ships, *Köln* and *Mainz*. And then just two days ago a pre-*Scharnhorst* armored cruiser, *Yorck*, hit a mine in home waters and sunk while getting out of the way for Germany's four battle cruisers, which were returning from an ill-advised raid on Yarmouth. Two hundred and fifty sailors drowned.

Shaken by these disasters, Wilhelm ordered his main battle fleet of thirteen dreadnoughts to stay in port rather than risking defeat in the North Sea against Britain's twenty-two dreadnoughts and five battle cruisers. He did this even though five or six of the enemy's big ships were unavailable on any given day because rigorous blockade duty had necessitated dry dock or repairs. Wilhelm would not hear of a Detached Division putting to sea either—not even a lone battle cruiser. The German naval attaché in San Francisco, having requested one of these fast capital ships to help Graf Spee get home, was told this was "impossible." If victory came soon, the Kaiser's expensive warships would remain in tact. If the war ended as it was now, stuck in stalemate, he still had *all* of the powerful home fleet as bargaining chip at a peace conference.

Chief of the Naval Staff Hugo von Pohl supported this decision, but Germany's famous Naval Minister, Alfred von Tirpitz, vehemently opposed political arguments that he saw as a proxy for other sentiments, namely, cowardice. Since the outbreak of war he had

stayed in close orbit to the Kaiser in a failing bid to bolster the resolve of the All Highest.

•   •   •

"Yes, Alfred, it's quite true. Müller called this morning, and says His Majesty's depression over loss of the
Yorck has turned to manic excitement. He awarded
all officers and crewmen of the *Emden* the Iron Cross.
As for Graf Spee's glorious victory over the Royal Navy:
hundreds more Iron Crosses, and every church bell in
Germany is to peal out the good tidings."

"Well, I am *so* pleased that the Kaiser's spirits are
up," said Tirpitz sarcastically. "Why, we can't have
the Supreme Warlord in a down mood can we?" he
added as both laughed—but Tirpitz much more than
Pohl—in a way making it very clear that the military,
not the Kaiser, was in control of this war.

"Now Hugo, to business if we may."

"Of course," said Pohl. "The *Emden* is on her own,
and from all of the reports, commanded superbly by
Captain Müller. We don't need to discuss her. As for
the rest of the squadron, I've already advised Spee
against cruiser warfare on the trade routes of South
America—he won't have enough coal. He should
break for home."

"Yes, and avoid another engagement. He may not
have enough shells after Coronel to fight a second
battle and then a third in the Channel or North Sea."

Pohl nodded agreement, and Tirpitz continued.

"We have news of an English squadron that has
formed near Montevideo. Exactly how strong we don't

know, or what else they may be sending south, but I propose that you *order him* to avoid the east coast of Argentina and head north through the middle of the Atlantic. Sailing his ships through these vast tracts, they have a decent chance of getting through the blockade. Sometimes I think it would take a miracle, but on sober reflection, he really does have a good chance."

"I agree with most of what you propose, but I won't *order it*. He must be given the discretion to judge for himself what the best course of action is. The Kaiser laid out guidelines for the autonomy of overseas commanders very clearly before the war."

"*You* should take the initiative! You're the one who's really in command here!" Tirpitz looked as if he wanted to press his point further, but a stern glance of disapproval from Pohl stopped him cold—for Pohl, not Tirpitz, had operational control, as long as the Kaiser approved.

"Well," Tirpitz finally continued, "at least we agree that Spee should make the attempt. And if he succeeds, the prestige won at Coronel, his apparent invincibility, will again be demonstrated for the whole world to see, as will the evident vulnerability of the Royal Navy."

Tirpitz stopped talking briefly to gather himself for the main point.

"Pin pricks like the Yarmouth raid are not enough. For months I have said the fleet must go out, and I've gotten nowhere. All the advantage in the North Sea goes to those who hold the initiative. We should seize it, just like *Emden* and *Karlsruhe* are doing. But now the British hold the initiative, and the longer this war lasts, the more her hunger blockade will eliminate Germany's chances of winning."

He paused again, glaring at Pohl, who over the past two months he had already sized up as a weakling and a mountebank—a cowardly sycophant.

"But consider this: if Graf Spee succeeds in reinforcing the High Seas Fleet with *Scharnhorst* and *Gneisenau*, this will surely be the moment to accept action in the North Sea. We now augment our battle cruiser squadron with *Blücher*, the only modern armored cruiser in the home fleet. If the East Asiatic gets back, that's *three* armored cruisers, four battle cruisers, and thirteen dreadnoughts—Germany will have twenty capital ships against twenty-one or so, or fewer if the English have detached ships to get revenge for Coronel. What's more, our ships have thicker armor, our range finders and fire control systems are better, and Graf Spee's gunners are the best in the world. Who could deny that we would be strong enough to defeat or at least do substantial injury to their so-called Grand Fleet?"

Pohl still did not look impressed, so Tirpitz pressed forward.

"Even if the battle is indecisive, neutral nations like Italy, which hesitate to throw in with us now out of fear of Britain's maritime superiority, will reconsider their neutrality. And think of the impact in the Muslim world! The *Emden* sparked a minor uprising with one ship at Madras: a major victory or good fight at sea would really awaken the Indians, the Egyptians, and others. We—the navy, not the army—have it in our grasp to bring England down!"

While Tirpitz spoke, his peroration rising to a high pitch, Pohl lit a cigar and listened, still clearly unimpressed—he looked annoyed, in fact, trying unsuccessfully a few times to get a word in. But when the Naval Minister finished, Pohl finally got his chance to reply.

"The Kaiser, Privy Naval Counselor Müller, and Chancellor Bethmann Hollweg will not have it! How many times has Bethmann impressed upon me the absolute necessity of preserving the fleet intact until the conclusion of peace?! We need an undamaged fleet at the peace table as leverage against England!"

But Tirpitz, who was already questioning the legitimacy of the current monarch—and therefore, implicitly or explicitly, the legitimacy of the monarchical system—*absolutely* had to get in the last word.

"Hugo, listen to me. If Graf Spee reaches close to home safely and the fleet doesn't go out, if we condemn our own noble sailors to death, the German nation will never forgive its sovereign. But let's be serious. You know as well as I that if Spee makes it back, with his standing in the navy, not to mention his standing in the public eye, you will need only ten minutes with our waffling emperor to talk the so-called All-Highest into taking the whole damn fleet into the North Sea to rescue our valiant East Asiatic Squadron and destroy the enemy fleet at the same time! *Carthaga delenda est!*"

Tirpitz had invoked the memory of antiquity, whose patina of glory still covered much of German officialdom in 1914. Roman general Scipio Africanus had said: "Carthage must be destroyed", and Rome, a land power, had finally accomplished this after three terrible wars. But was Germany, a land power, in a position to repeat history, ancient history, and bring an end to the naval rule of Britannia? Tirpitz thought so, and he was counting on the return of Graf Maximilian von Spee to help swing the political argument in favor of finally sending out the High Seas Fleet to defeat mighty Britain.

"Very well," said the tired navy chief. "I'll advise Spee that the fleet will come out to meet him when his squadron gets close enough. And you're right—when the moment arrives, I shall probably encounter little opposition from the Kaiser."

XVII
MÁS AFUERA

Scharnhorst, Gneisenau, and *Nürnberg* quitted the roadstead of Valparaiso on the morning of November 4th, three grey ships in a proud line.[13] As we departed, the peers and jetties were lined with our compatriots, hats waving farewells. They had plied us with flowers and presents of every kind, and we were so profoundly touched, for it was not easy being cut off from the Fatherland in its hour of need—a fate they shared with us. But the farewell waves evoked a kind of melancholia among the officers, whose mood had by now darkened. Indeed our fellow Germans on shore seemed to know as well as we did that the next battle would not be so easy, and to sense that the East Asiatic might be setting out on its last cruise.

At first light on November 6th, a Friday, the squadron found itself nearing its old anchorage against the giant rocks of Más Afuera. All were disconsolate. No one knew which course we would set next, and what awaited us there. We had only coaling to look forward to, which was not the glorious feat of arms that many of our new recruits expected when they came on board.

---

13   From Pochhammer, *Before Jutland.* See my methodological Afterword.

The following Friday the 13th, that unlucky day, found us still beneath the cliffs. We were once again small ships, looking constantly up at rocks so much more impressive than we. For a week the captains had met one-on-one with the admiral, trying to convince him to move—anything was better than these Pygmy ships resting demoralizingly at anchor! And then that afternoon the admiral signaled that all of the top offi-cers should assemble in his conference room aboard the flagship to determine our destiny. It was high time, for morale was sinking! Would the decision bring us good fortune—or bad?

• • •

Having welcomed his officers to the conference, Spee asked all to be seated. He remained standing, walked over to his wall map, picked up the pointer, and turned back toward his squadron commanders and first officers. "In the last few days many of you have expressed your opinions to me privately concerning our next course of action."

He turned around to use the map. "Some favor seeking shelter in the remote South Atlantic, perhaps in South Georgia. Others have urged steaming for Africa to protect our colonies there, or even rounding the Cape into the Indian Ocean to gather up *Königsberg* off East Africa and eventually reunite with *Emden*. A third idea expressed is to round the Horn and throw the shipping lanes off Argentina into a panic."

"One thing is certain," he continued, walking back to the table and sitting down, "we can't remain here."

He took a dispatch out of a folder in front of him. "Our naval attaché in San Francisco urges us 'to leave immediately' as we are 'dangerously situated.' The Japanese have a battle cruiser lurking, and the *Australia* may soon appear out of nowhere. As you know, I have favored making a break for home, although the coaling difficulties of another long cruise, not to mention our half-empty magazines, gave me pause. Now, without issuing strict orders, Admiralty has made our decision easier. Two dispatches from Berlin over Valparaiso have reached me."

Graf Spee took the communiqués out of his portfolio and summarized the first: "The first reminds us of the presence of light cruiser *Karlsruhe* in the Caribbean, implying that we have a better chance of reaching the Fatherland if she augments the squadron. Indeed, she is faster and more heavily armed than any of our light cruisers—and carries mines, which could guard our rear in the Channel."

"The second provides more detailed recommendations: 'It is left to your discretion to break off cruiser warfare against trade and attempt to break through to Germany. You may succeed if your preparations are accompanied by good luck. The best course would be, if possible, to penetrate the Royal Navy's dispersed lines of trade protection in the North Atlantic, operating suddenly so that enemy cruisers are not concentrated against you. Once closer to Germany bear in mind that strong enemy blockade patrols in the English Channel and North Sea can only be broken through with the assistance of the home fleet; therefore your intentions should be communicated early. Signed:

Admiral Hugo von Pohl, Chief of the Naval Staff, High Seas Fleet.' "

"I have drafted the following reply: 'The East Asiatic Squadron intends to break through for home.' "

"What is your view of the situation gentlemen?"

Before anyone could reply the flagship's communications officer entered the caucus unexpectedly and said in a loud, crisp voice: "Excuse me, sir, but we have news of *Emden*." Spee immediately crossed the room, took the message into his hand, and began to read it.

XVIII
PANANG

Eichhorn spoke the truth when he told Graf Spee that *Emden*'s skipper had already carved out a place for himself in history. However, as the ambitious, noble corsair left his remote lair at Diego Garcia on the morning of October 10th he was about to descend deeper into the realm of legend. Müller's plan, formulated painstakingly while pouring over the charts and bits of intelligence that he had, was to raid the port of Panang, far off to the east in British Malaya.

Three days out to sea steaming north toward Ceylon, however, his communications officer, Guérard, rushed to the captain with a wireless intercept: an English steamer en route from Aden to Ceylon had been assured by the Royal Navy that the passage was now safe. So Müller changed plans and headed for his new whaling ground off the southwest coast of India.

In four and a half days, October 15th to 19th, *Emden* proved that this route was anything but "safe." She captured seven ships, sinking all but one, the *Exford*, loaded with 5,500 tons of the best coal in the world. Fuel would not be a problem for the German pirates, who had now sunk or taken twenty-one enemy merchant ships. Unless the British got lucky, it looked as if the unimaginably vast spaces of the Indian Ocean would provide ample hiding places for Müller's flotilla. To the aggravation of Churchill and the Admiralty, there seemed to be no end to this self-perpetuating preying on and disruption of British shipping.

Not wanting to push his luck by continuing to hunt in the same waters, Müller broke off the kill on October 20th, embarked on a wide southerly sweep around Ceylon, and finally headed east toward Penang. He freed a mass of well-fed, grateful captives aboard a ship seized earlier. Like other passengers and crew members liberated before them, this throng of six hundred cheered the gallantry of their captors.

As the Germans steamed south and then east across the Bay of Bengal, coal was taken on at sea with the usual difficulty and the same risk to attack. By the time they rounded the northern coast of Sumatra and entered the Malacca Strait, a day out of Penang, the colliers had been detached, one by one, to designated rendezvous points. Early on the morning of October 27th *Emden* increased speed to fifteen knots in order to enter the harbor at first light on the morrow. A few hours later Müller assembled his officers in the wardroom to lay out his plan of attack.

•   •   •

The captain entered and motioned that all, who were standing at attention, take their seats. "Gentlemen, it is time that we stopped being the hunted. Tomorrow I intend to do some hunting of my own. The English and their allies use Penang as one of their search bases. If we succeed in achieving surprise, we'll catch enemy warships at anchor and torpedo them. Enemy merchant ships also using Penang as a haven will each receive a few well-placed cannon shots at the waterline. With luck we can do as much damage to enemy commerce in one morning—or maybe even more damage—as we have inflicted over the last six weeks."

At 1700 hours the order piped through scores of speaking tubes: "All hands aft!" Müller wanted his men ready for anything with high morale. Once the crew minus those on watch assembled he walked to the back of the quarterdeck and raised a hand to command silence.

"Men of Germany, men of the *Emden*! Thus far we have brought honor and glory to the city whose name this ship bears. But who among you has not grown tired of destroying defenseless steamers, which is quite all right, but no deed of arms to make men like us properly proud—men of the sea, who among you does not long to test his mettle against enemy men-of-war?!"

As their captain said this, the sailors looked at one another excitedly, and then cheered. Müller again raised his hand for silence.

"Tomorrow I shall give you that chance. I intend to raid the English base at Penang and destroy all ships flying the flags of nations at war with Germany. Your officers will be issuing your orders. I know that you will fight bravely when the moment for action arrives! You will do your duty faithfully and bring honor to the Fatherland!"

The cheering broke out again even louder than before.

• • •

Müller and Mücke stood on the bridge as the island of Palau-Penang, its harbor lights unsuspectingly glowing in the early morning darkness, came into view. The *Emden* turned hard to starboard, skirted the island, and entered westward into the narrow, thousand-yard channel leading to the port and ships at anchor.

The time was 0450 hours, October 28th, 1914. Far, far, far to the east, half way around the world, Graf Spee's squadron raised steam in Más Afuera to speed toward its destiny off Chile. In a few hours Christopher Cradock would receive a wireless from *Glasgow* that doomed 1,600 men of the Royal Navy. Müller, as if telepathically signaling his desire to fight the same fight as his admiral, firmly but calmly gave orders for battle: "Raise the dummy funnel. Clear the ship for action. Stand ready."

All hands sprang to their stations: Müller went below to the armored coning tower, Mücke ascended into his observation perch in the foremast, Prince Franz Joseph Hohenzollern descended into the torpedo room, his friend Levetzow raced to his portside aft 4.1-inch gun, and Guérard ran into the radio room. Lauterbach, his special services not needed in this battle, observed what was about to happen from behind a starboard battery amidships.

Shortly after 0500 Mücke yelled into his speaking tube: "Russian light cruiser four points to starboard!" Müller had noticed the lights of this vessel too, and soon three masts, three funnels, and numerous gun mounts came into focus. He turned to Gaede and ordered: "Ready starboard torpedo tube, ready starboard batteries." The order was relayed electronically to these stations.

At 0517, with only four hundred yards between the ships, the order "fire" appeared on the torpedo room telegraph and Hohenzollern launched *Emden*'s starboard torpedo. A moment later it crashed into the stern of the targeted ship, the *Chemtchug*, with a deafeningly loud report, sending flames, smoke, and debris high into the air. Crippled by a heavy-caliber projectile seventeen and a half inches thick and packed with high explosives, the stricken enemy ship settled into the water and sunk astern to deck level. The element of surprise now gone, top flags were raised, all starboard guns of the *Emden* opened fire on the forecastle, and then, as quickly as the crews could reload, second and third salvos went into the water line. The *Chemtchug* blazed as some of her startled crew that had survived jumped overboard.

From his armored tower Müller noticed that *Emden* closed fast on all sorts of merchant ships anchored in the harbor, so he ordered: "Hard to port, ready port torpedo tube." The German raider was turning about to finish off the Russian cruiser.

At seven hundred yards a second deadly torpedo struck, causing an even greater and more violent explosion—her magazine hit, the *Chemtchug* lifted high into the air and broke in two inside a yellowish, greenish cloud. When the cordite smoke cleared, three masts protruding out of shallow water hinted sorrowfully at what moments earlier had been a proud warship. Ninety-one Russians perished; one hundred and eight had terrible wounds—half of the crew, casualties.

Not able to ponder this victory for long lest he ignore his duties, Mücke noticed a ship bearing down on them at full speed enshrouded in smoke from its laboring engines. He barked down: "Smoke dead ahead!"

The skipper yanked his binoculars from the remains of the *Chemtchug* to inspect what approached. "All ahead full," he commanded. *Emden* speeded up as it went back into the channel it had entered less than an hour earlier. Smoke still hid the enemy's identity, but Müller, taking no chances that she get away a first salvo, ordered the bow guns to fire at 6,000 yards. Hit and holed, taking on water badly, dead sailors strewn all over her, the victim, an unarmed government patrol boat, limped to shore and went aground to avoid sinking. Shell-shocked survivors aboard the unfortunate vessel started to tend to the wounded. "Cease fire" reverberated through *Emden*.

It was now too risky to reenter Panang and sink merchant ships. A destroyer had been spotted; torpedo boats could be there too; and either could take out a cruiser if they got close enough. Disappointed that he had not inflicted more harm on the enemy, Müller ordered the Swan of the East north to port once out of the channel.

With Penang ten miles behind the raider and *Emden* now a mile from shore, Mücke, who had stayed aloft, once again announced an approaching ship to starboard. This time the first officer had spotted a warship, the French destroyer *Mousquet*. Not willing to give the smaller ship a chance for a torpedo run, Müller commenced fire with the starboard batteries at 4,700 yards, blowing away the French flag and exploding the boiler, which emitted a huge cloud of white steam. As successive salvos slammed into the *Mousquet*, crewmen were hurled overboard, many others blown to pieces—forty-two brave sailors died.

The captain's feet had been ripped away, but in his last moments of consciousness, bleeding to death, he insisted on being lashed to the mast. Desperately fighting back, the dying French skipper turned his injured ship to port and fired a torpedo that missed. Müller ordered a coup de grace salvo, which brought the destroyer to a dead stop in the water. A minute later she went down by the bow and sank perpendicularly, her captain's dead body visible until the last, all-final plunge into the deep. As the deceased victim disappeared beneath the waves, his right arm, raised seconds earlier for its last command, flopped downward as if beckoning hated German foes to follow.

Emden fished thirty surviving Frenchmen out of the sea and sped north. The Battle of Penang was over.

XIX
THE COCOS ISLANDS

Three days later, having gone westward back around the northern tip of Sumatra, stopped a British steamer, and offloaded French prisoners onto her, Müller rendezvoused with his best collier, the *Buresk*. From her he learned the British had captured two of his colliers, *Markomannia* and *Pontoporos*. They had little coal left, so this was not a major setback, but two score of his sailors that operated these ships were now in captivity.

Because the much more valuable *Exford* waited in rendezvous north of the Cocos Islands, just off the Australia-to-India shipping lane, he headed toward her. On November 1st, the very day Graf Spee sunk Cradock's cruisers, Müller steamed off the west coast of Sumatra. After prowling unsuccessfully for a day farther south in the straits above Java, he set a southwesterly course out to sea for the prearranged meeting place with *Exford*.

Underway a half day from the Cocos at dusk on November 7th, an odd incident occurred. Lauterbach stood watch on the roof of the bridge as the sun descended lazily in the western sky. Suddenly a giant albatross landed on the aft-side railing, startling the burly prize officer so badly that he almost fell over

189

backwards. The jet black intruder with a white head spread its wings to their full span of thirteen feet, opened its imposing crooked beak, and squawked loudly and menacingly.

Lauterbach quickly pulled himself together. "So, my *little* friend, are you hungry for some good German food—*Delicat Essen*?" he said, bowing as if a waiter. Lauterbach turned to a nearby sailor and ordered him to bring scraps from the galley.

This done, the albatross began to feed itself. Lauterbach enjoyed this so much that he wanted the other officers in the ward room to come see, so the sailor was ordered below to summon them.

Now, assuming the pose of some famous actor, and pausing only briefly to remember the correct verses, *Emden*'s overweight thespian began to recite from Samuel Taylor Coleridge's "Rime of the Ancient Mariner." Lauterbach seemed perfectly content performing to an audience of one big bird.

"At length did cross an Albatross:
Through the fog it came;
As if it had been a Christian soul,
We hailed it in God's name.

It ate the food it ne'er had eat,
And round and round it flew.
The ice did split with a thunder-fit;
The helmsman steered us through!

And a good south wind sprung up behind;
The Albatross did follow,

And every day, for food or play,
Came to the mariners' hollo!

In mist or cloud, on mast or shroud,
It perched for vespers nine;
Whiles all the night, through fog-smoke white,
Glimmered the white Moonshine."

Meanwhile, Lauterbach's messenger reached the wardroom. There sat Mücke, Gaede, Hohenzollern, Levetzow, and Guérard. "The officer of the watch wishes to report that there is a giant albatross topside— it's a big-ass *Dösskopp!*"

Mücke had already downed a few. The unfriendly first officer leaned forward and responded to the messenger in a cruel tone: "Our compliments to the officer of the watch, but tell him we've known for hours that we had a big-ass *Dösskopp* on the bridge." All roared with laughter, and then drank a toast—with double meaning—to the *Dösskopp*, which is German for albatross.

When the sailor returned and reported this, Lauterbach understood that once again his bulk was the butt of jokes, but he laughed too, as was his jolly nature.

Presently, Mücke and the others marched up to see. The *Dösskopp* still gorged itself on disgusting-looking galley scraps. Suddenly Mücke stepped toward the bird, spread his arms like wings, and shouted: "Be gone, ugly black thing!" This so startled the unsuspecting bird that it took off, flying up and to the back. One of its wings slammed against the foremast directly behind the bridge platform. Clearly hurt but not crippled, the albatross struggled along its way.

The commotion above stirred Müller, who had been resting on Lauterbach's chair in the chartroom behind the bridge below. He rubbed his eyes and then ascended to the observation platform. "What goes on?" he inquired.

Lauterbach remained silent—he was not at all amused by what Mücke had done. But the first officer replied to the captain calmly and confidently: "Just a *Dösskopp*, captain. I scared it away."

In an angry, glaring tone this time, Lauterbach resumed his oration:

"And I had done an hellish thing,
And it would work 'em woe;
For all averred, I had killed the bird
That made the breeze to blow,
Ah wretch! said they, the bird to slay
That made the breeze to blow."

As Lauterbach spoke his barbed piece of poetry, Mücke grew more and more agitated. It was partly the drink at work, but also his hatred for the English, even their language. But Müller held up his hand as if ordering that his valuable prize officer be allowed to finish. With the stanza finished, however, he stopped Lauterbach in English: "No more silliness from you—get below, and the rest of you too." The captain temporarily took over the watch himself.

Now it is well known that men of the sea are very superstitious. To some of the old salts on *Emden* the strange visit was, in and of itself, an evil omen, for giant black albatrosses, they said, were harbingers of bad luck. But others disagreed: the albatross brought good luck, but to mistreat it so was to tempt fate. Either way, the mood among the men was not good—bad, in fact.

· · ·

It seemed like nothing at the time, but to this day I cannot put the bizarre encounter with the albatross out of my mind, for from that moment forward our luck, very good until then, changed. Was it simply because the big bird had perched on my ship that turned things around? Or was it the impetuous behavior of my first officer in injuring the big black creature? Guérard brought the grumbling of the crew, which expressed this side and that, to my attention. Or had we just been much too lucky already, and now things had to change? Whatever the case, our luck ran out—totally and quickly out, as if we were cursed.

That evening I wanted to rendezvous with *Exford*, but she was nowhere to be found. All night long we searched in vain for our second collier, but it was not until late morning of the next day, Sunday, November 8th, that we found the ship. This was most unfortunate because I was forced to postpone *Emden*'s next action until first light on November 9th, the best time of day to achieve surprise.

I hoped that our descent on Penang and continued presence in Sumatran waters would lure English search sweeps eastward. As further bait I planned to raid the

Cocos Islands to destroy an English wireless station and oceanic cables. This would also disrupt Royal Navy communications in the region—we knew that a large troop convoy had sailed from Australia and New Zealand. Afterwards, with the enemy scouring the southeast, we would race across the expanses of the Indian Ocean to take prizes off the Horn of Africa. We had heard nothing of SMS *Königsberg*, so English patrols must have caught up with her—we learned in captivity that they had indeed trapped her in the Rufigi River of East Africa. I transferred Lauterbach, much against his will, to *Exford* on November 8th and ordered him to sail for the Horn.

As it turned out, the ANZAC convoy *had* been thereabouts on the morning I wanted to make the attack. It cruised maintaining radio silence 150 nautical miles southeast of the Cocos heading northwest toward Ceylon—a good six or seven hours away for a fast cruiser. The only radio signals we picked up that day, and again on the morning of our landing, were, it appeared from the weakness of the signal, 250 miles away. Grant cleared up their origin for us— they came from the convoy's flagship, HMS *Minotaur*, which Churchill had detached westward to suppress an uprising of Dutch Boers in South Africa.

Although we did not know it, however, there were indeed warships only 50 miles from the Cocos on November 9th. Despite the slow speed of the massive convoy, it covered almost 200 miles, progressing from southeast of the islands to a position northwest of them, all this while *Emden* dawdled another day at sea waiting to make the attack—enemy warships more powerful than ours only two hours away!

· · ·

On the evening of November 8th Müller convened his officers to explain the morrow's attack, which he wanted Mücke and fifty hand-picked navy veterans to execute, many of them selected from the gunners and crews of the main gun mounts to reward them with a few diversionary hours ashore for their good marksmanship during the Penang raid. Obviously the captain did not anticipate a battle, either on the island, or what would be worse, at sea. He had only a little steam up in eight of his twelve boilers. The only action of any sort that he planned was to take on coal from *Buresk* after his landing party was back. He thought he had all day.

Gaede, the gunnery officer, questioned the wisdom of sending his best gunners ashore: "If we get into a scrap, sir, there will be the devil to pay."

"There's a risk, certainly, but only a small one. The island is not defended. The closest enemy ship is a day away and its signals are growing weaker—probably heading south or west. Besides, our landing party will be back on board in three hours."

But Gaede, backed up by Guérard, persisted: "With all due respect, captain, wouldn't it be better to bombard the island and then steal away?"

"Yes," said the ship's radio officer, "the wireless operators won't have any time to send an SOS."

"No. I've considered this and decided against bombarding. Too many civilians could be killed, which will blacken the name of our ship and tar the honor of the Fatherland." And then, turning to Mücke, Müller gave his final orders: "Select the rest of the landing party, assemble your weapons, and be away by 0600. You must be back by 0900. Carry on, gentlemen."

At the appointed hour, Mücke reported to the bridge. Wearing summer whites, having donned a topee hat to shield him from the tropical sun, he saluted Müller, and then descended from the port side of *Emden* into the launch that would tow two cutters to shore. The landing party was heavily armed with revolvers, rifles, the ship's four machine guns, and explosive charges. The three landing vessels loaded on the seaward, northern port side to block observation from the island until they got underway.

Already before they came into view, however, the element of surprise had begun to slip away. A Chinese servant saw the warship offshore and told a wireless operator who was coming out of the station just before 0600. The operator, joined a few minutes later by the superintendent, climbed up to the roof and took a closer look through binoculars—flying no flags, with its somewhat odd-looking fake fourth funnel, the visitor had to be the *Emden*. By the time Mücke's men covered the mile to the island at 0630 and then began to execute their mission, the wireless station had been sending and resending the same message for fifteen minutes: "SOS. *Emden* here … SOS. *Emden* here."

It took only a half hour for the noose to tighten around the neck of Müller and his men. *Minotaur*, steaming rapidly to the west, received the SOS and immediately warned the flagship of the convoy, light cruiser HMAS *Melbourne* of the Royal Australian Navy, commanded by Captain Mortimer Silver, who had little time to make a tough decision.

Under Silver's command sailed the massive Japanese battle cruiser *Ibuki*, boasting a powerful array of 12- and 8-inch guns. Her commander, Captain Kato, had also received *Minotaur*'s warning and quickly ordered a signalman to flag a message to *Melbourne*: "Request the honor of sinking the German raider." Kato took it as an insult to his nation, however, when his wish was not granted: Silver, wanting a ship of the British Empire to destroy *Emden*, signaled his second light cruiser, HMAS *Sydney*, with Captain John Glossop at the helm, to reverse course and steam ahead full for the Cocos. Her superior speed and 6-inch guns should guarantee victory. She pealed away from the convoy at 0700.

Meanwhile, *Emden*'s raiding party had been going about its business, rounding up the station personnel, exploding the tall wireless mast, setting explosive charges on a few vessels in the harbor, and—what proved most time-consuming—locating the underwater telegraph cables, laboriously breaking them apart, dragging them out of the sea, and then throwing them overboard far away from shore. An hour passed, then two, and still Mücke's teams had not finished.

Müller looked anxiously at his watch, then the island, then his watch again: 0900 and still no sign of the landing party heading back to the ship. Suddenly a lookout in the top mast yelled out: "Smoke four points off the port bow!" The captain and Guérard, who had taken over for Mücke, walked onto the seaward flying bridge to investigate. "It could be the *Buresk*," said Müller, "she's due here in an hour."

They waited and watched as the minutes ticked by. "What is keeping Mücke?!" blurted the angry skipper. "Sound the siren to recall them from the island."

At 0915, just as the siren blasted three times, the signal for dropping everything and double-timing back, the ship approaching rapidly from the northwest turned two points south and came away from the smoke cloud that hung around her. What came into better view was not *Buresk*, but rather the tall masts of a four-funneled warship flying white battle ensigns bearing the Cross of St. George—this was an Australian light cruiser.

Without a second's hesitation Müller issued his orders in staccato succession: "Full steam in all boilers. Weigh anchor. All ahead full. Hoist the top flags. Clear the ship for action. Load torpedo tubes." Drum rolls and alarm bells sent each man hurriedly to his station.

Müller inspected all of this from his flying bridge for a moment as a startled look came over his face. Desperate thoughts raced through his mind: "No steam, no first officer, none of my best gun-layers, fifty of my best men ashore—it's all the work of the devil."

He had only a split second to curse these adverse circumstances, however, before descending into the armored tower to join his chief gunnery officer, his chief torpedo officer, the combat helmsman, and a few petty officers and sailors. Guérard, whose analysis of the impending calculus of battle was not as astute, saluted his captain with an enthusiastic, combative look about him and then climbed into the first officer's perch in the foremast.

The captain picked up a speaking tube and fired a question down to the chief engineer below in the mines. "How long before you can get me anything close to full speed?" He listened to the answer, hung up, and swore: "Damn it all to hell. I don't have an hour!"

Mücke, in the meantime, had assembled his men as quickly as possible and herded them into the boats. As the launch started chugging, towing its charges out of the harbor, however, he observed *Emden* hoist the "Weigh-Anchor" flag, and moments later, take off, slowly picking up speed and pulling away from them to the northwest. His team all waved and shouted for the mother ship to wait, but she did not. S o m e t h i n g was obviously wrong. Mücke did not know what for a few minutes, but at 0930 he saw what Müller had noticed before: to his right an enemy cruiser barrel-ing at top speed to the south. The hunter suddenly turned hard to starboard and charged at the slower German vessel for a few minutes, then tacked hard to starboard again. It was 0940 and both ships, still over 10,000 yards apart, moved northwestwardly in parallel battle line.

"Salvos fire!" barked Müller to Gaede. Both, already looking to starboard, saw the menacing flash of *Syd-ney*'s guns, and seconds later, *Emden*'s first five shells going a few hundred yards over. Guérard dutifully yelled this into his speaking tube.

Almost simultaneously enemy shells splashed far off to port, sending water spouts high into the air. "6-inch shells," said Gaede alarmingly.

"Tell me something I don't know, Gaede. Fire again when ready!" And to close the distance he told the helmsman: "Two points to starboard."

Emden fired her second and third broadsides while *Sydney* struggled to find the range. The second again went over, but twenty seconds later the third scored several direct hits. The German gun crews cheered wildly, and Gaede, eager to give his captain good news, reported proudly: "Sir, we've taken out their forward fire control station!" A moment later Guérard from his better vantage point announced that the rear fire control mast had also been hit.

On board *Sydney*, the German shell crashed into the forecastle area with a thudding sound—it caused damage but did not explode. The skipper, struggling to his feet, alertly ordered: "All guns to commence manual fire." Turning to his first officer, who had clearly been frightened by this lucky cheating of death, Glossop inquired: "What damage aft?"

His Number One walked to the starboard captain's bridge, looked back, and reported: "The mast is damaged, but it should have been worse. His shells are not bursting properly."

Struggling to instantly process all of this audio and visual information, Müller knew something did not add up. *Emden* desperately needed to destroy the enemy quickly before his firepower and speed swung the battle around. These hits were therefore welcome, but not the lack of damage to *Sydney*. "Our shells cannot possibly be detonating, Gaede. Have all crews double-check that fuse caps are set to detonate."

Sydney had been forced to fire its guns manually, and not surprisingly continued to miss—even Mücke, far away in his launch, commented: "The enemy ship fires very badly."

As the minutes passed until 1000, with both combatants still about 9,000 yards apart, *Emden* got away five more salvos, the last slamming into the aft starboard gun mount and starting a fire. Seeing this, Müller's eyes widened but then quickly narrowed in disappointment. He had expected *Sydney*'s rear magazine to blow—and it had not. "Even at this distance and barrel elevation we should be doing more harm, Gaede."

A shocked look came over the captain's face. "For Christ's sake, Gaede, the damned gun crews didn't reverse the cap screws on the fuses. Our shells are on safety!" As Gaede again responded into a speaking tube to the gunners, Müller turned to the helmsman: "Two more points to starboard!" Into the speaking tube to the engine room he ordered: "Give me more steam!" Already 1005 hours, and *Emden* still had nothing close to full speed.

Just as the furious, frustrated Müller issued these orders, a 6-inch shell hit the radio room amidships, obliterating it and killing all inside. Another exploded near the foremast, blowing away the arm of a petty officer. A third hit directly in front of the armored conning tower, tearing apart the bodies of most of the men of the two bow gun crews, whose shields, facing forward, provided no protection. The explosion did not harm those inside around the captain, but blood spewed threw the slits and spattered all of them.

Now that the Australian had the range the Battle of the Cocos Islands grew ever more lopsided. Its next salvo knocked over the forward funnel, whose stays had been removed in preparation for coaling from the Buresk. Another shrapnel shell detonated right in front of the forecastle, finishing off the gun crews there and spraying splinters into the conning tower and lightly wounding all but Müller. The third hit wrecked even greater havoc, exploding between the stern gun crews in a stack of thirty shells, shaking the whole ship, igniting a huge fire, and inflicting the same carnage as earlier on the bow: sixteen men were dismembered, including Levetzow.

Additional hits came one after another every few seconds now, and as the minutes passed, less and less remained undamaged on the once elegant Swan of the East. The second and third funnels were knocked over. The foremast was blown up, killing Guérard and his signalman as it crashed into the sea. The shell hoists to the magazines were all wrecked. Most of the gun crews, as well as the replacements who rushed to the mounts to keep up fire, were killed or badly wounded. The same grisly fate had been meted out to the shell carriers. Even most of those in the conning tower had been killed. After first the electronic fire control and then most of the speaking tubes had been destroyed, Gaede and the others, with no useful role left there, rushed out onto the deck to do what they could and died almost instantly.

With little else to fight with by 1025 hours, and only the helmsman left in the forecastle, Müller ordered: "Hard to port." Into a speaking tube (that he hoped was working) he yelled: "Ready starboard tube."

Observing the turning tide of battle helplessly from afar, Mücke changed plans. Rather than trying to catch *Emden*, he ordered his mini-fleet back to shore. A schooner they had placed charges aboard earlier was commandeered, all available supplies and provisions hurriedly brought aboard, and the vessel made ready for departure. The first officer hoped to escape in order to fight another day for his Fatherland. Not a likeable person, he was certainly no coward.

While Mücke loaded the schooner, which could not be done quickly, the sea battle rushed ineluctably to its violent conclusion. Every time *Emden* tried to close the distance for more effective fire from her novice gun layers, or to make a torpedo run, *Sydney* tacked defensively and maintained her distance. She could make twenty-seven knots, but the German cruiser, with all funnels down and some damage in the engine rooms, still struggled to approach twenty.

Finally, at about 1100 hours, with the torpedo flat flooded and his last option therefore gone, Müller veered off to port and hobbled directly for a small coral reef island. He would run *Emden* aground, prevent her from sinking, and save as many remaining lives as possible.

Seeing this apparent escape attempt, *Sydney* fired salvos in rapid succession, turning *Emden*'s superstructure into an even greater tangle of burning metal and killing many more German sailors. By this point Müller had lost almost a third of the men on board—a hundred officers and sailors. Another twenty had terrible wounds. Finally *Emden* reached the reef off the island, screeching, scraping, and lurching slightly to a halt. Frustrated, *Sydney* sped away to the north to overtake the *Buresk*, which had been spotted trying to escape.

Wreck of the *Emden*: "Water, water everywhere ... Nor any drop to drink"
(Hohenzollern, *Emden*)

The anguishing Battle of the Cocos Islands appeared to be over—mercifully, tragically over. But oftentimes in war appearances can be deceptive—and this time, too, they were. More blood would be shed.

• • •

By now it was 1120 hours. Müller came out of his tower to inspect what was left of his ship. The terrible sight that awaited him brought a shocked, and then angry look to his face—the captain who had to succeed was mad at himself for bringing about Emden's fate.

Glancing to the rear, he saw Hohenzollern and his torpedo crew, who with great difficulty had found a way out of their flooded station and avoided drowning by only a few minutes. "Thank God you're all right," said Müller as the young prince approached. Luther, the ship's doctor, also emerged from the wreckage amidships, and together they organized teams of the able-bodied survivors to gather up all badly wounded men and deposit them on the forward deck, the only part of the ship that was not burning.

While Luther and a few sailors did what they could in their makeshift hospital, Müller issued a series of orders to his remaining officers and men. Fires were to be doused with seawater, the ship's code book, log, and other documents destroyed, all of the guns' breech-blocks removed and thrown overboard, gun sights smashed, and the magazines flooded. Nothing of military value should fall into enemy hands.

The crew soon encountered another enemy, however, that would also prove hard to defeat—thirst. Both the wounded and the unwounded, especially the former, were parched, but all of Emden's water tanks sat below decks in places either flooded or inaccessible because of the wreckage. Müller asked for volunteers to jump overboard, swim to the island—all of the ship's boats were either destroyed or still with Mücke—and gather milky coconuts. The "landing party" came forward and entered the very rough surf. Some of the fifteen could not swim well and drowned, while the razor-sharp reef eviscerated many of the others. As the ocean turned from benign blue to gory red, only three defeated, demoralized men got back on board.

From the island, meanwhile, eyes— enemy predator eyes— inspected their next meal. During the noisy storm of battle a colony of albatrosses that had probably nested there since time immemorial grew more and more agitated. Now the uninvited German guests who thirty-six hours earlier had been so boorish and rude would be taught nature's lesson in manners.

Three of the awesome winged things took off, circled the forward deck, and dove at their prey. One landed on Luther's shoulders and pecked a cheek apart, blood spewing all over his shirt. The others landed on two of the wounded, ripping at necks and feasting on eye balls. The agonizing, horrified cries of the ship's latest victims brought the nearest sailors running to the rescue, grabbing for any kind of available weapon—empty shell casings, pieces of the wreckage, and daggers, cudgels, and revolvers if they had them—and rushing back into battle.

The vicious birds proved determined opponents, however, and it took a second wave of *Emden* crewmen to kill or chase them away. This done, Müller posted an armed guard around the wounded. Other albatrosses were circling the ship by this time, threatening to dive, and it took repeated revolver volleys from the circled guard, commanded now by Hohenzollern as if in ground combat, to beat the attackers back to their island. The guard remained vigilant well into the afternoon.

· · ·

After a few hours passed, lookouts spotted smoke to the northeast. *Sydney* was returning, having failed to capture the *Buresk*, whose German crew scuttled the collier, abandoned ship, and surrendered. Would she help the German survivors? The victorious vessel approached *Emden*, passing 4,500 yards astern. The first officer turned to Glossop: "She's still flying top flags from the aft mast. This could be a trap."

Glossop was incredulous. "Surely not, she's aground with all her guns out of action."

"Sir, some of the German officers from *Buresk* have boasted that their captain will never surrender. If only one gun is able to get off a lucky hit … "

Glossop ordered a signal flagman: "Send: Will you surrender?"

The man relayed the German reply to his captain: "He says: Do not understand your signal. Have no codebook."

"Send the message in Morse with the signal light."

This was done, and all waited anxiously. "Sir, there is no reply."

Glossop and his first officer looked at one another alarmingly, but said nothing. After a few seconds the captain barked: "Open fire!"

The broadside shook *Emden* as if she had been hit by a powerful earthquake. Men, and arms, legs, and body trunks of men, were blown overboard—fifteen more were killed. The twisted metal superstructure of what had been a ship became even more hopelessly entangled. Müller, totally dumbfounded, ordered: "Save yourselves if you can swim." A handful of sailors did so, but fared no better on the blood-thirsty reef than their predecessors.

The shelling continued for five minutes. The galling scene presented war at its worst. Finally Müller noticed his battle ensigns flying aft, ordered a sailor to tear them down, grabbed some bandage material, and waved his improvised white flag desperately.

The murderous fire stopped immediately. On the bridge of the *Sydney* Glossop scowled at his Number One: "I could lose my stripes for this!"

"Surely not, sir, surely not."

·   ·   ·

War is war, however, and much worse acts of killing innocents or defenseless combatants would happen in this, the "Great War." The incident infuriated Müller, but Glossop did not lose his stripes.

And so, to the enormous relief of Churchill, the Royal Navy, and the entire allied shipping world, SMS *Emden* had finally been stopped. Captain Karl von Müller, Prince Hohenzollern, and other survivors accompanied the ANZAC convoy to Columbo, Ceylon, arriving there on Sunday, November 15th.

By this time Graf Spee had put to sea again, about to go down in history.

XX
PORT STANLEY

On HMS *Glasgow* we had no idea why the Germans had not pursued and destroyed us. We were glad they had not, but as our vessel, with battleship *Canopus* astern, sailed south, rounded a stormy Cape Horn, and turned north for Port Stanley, the collective mood could only be described as depressed. Never have I known the captain, officers, and men of a ship, all so closely knit that were so bound together in the sheer misery of a common tragedy. "A sure shield," the king had called the Royal Navy, and here we were a broken, bloody reed.[14]

First Officer Wilfred Thompson was a Godsend on that melancholy voyage. "It's high time we snapped out of this, chaps," he said one day, and then put the crew to work repairing the considerable damage done at Coronel: above decks a shambles; holed badly at the waterline; and the cabin of Captain Luce, where a shell had burst, a wreck.

As dawn broke on November 8th, one week after our disaster, the survivor ships passed the tall mast of the wireless station on Hooker's Point, neared Pembroke light house, turned hard a' port through Port William,

---

14 From Hickling, *Sailor at Sea*. See my methodological Afterword.

and finally into Stanley Harbor. I had to go into town to pick up dispatches. Thompson, who had also been ordered ashore to help organize the town's defenses, stood beside me. Although both down, I thought a little subtle humor might help. It was admittedly a feeble attempt.

• • •

"No women to greet us," said Higgs as he looked at a nearly motionless Stanley town.

Thompson smiled slightly, a polite acknowledgement of this stab at the upbeat in trying times. He took out a cigarette and began tapping it on his case. "After the atrocities in Belgium, Admiralty has probably ordered Governor Allardyce to evacuate the women and children." He kept tapping.

They saw no early morning activity except much of the 200-man Volunteer Defense Force digging fox holes and stacking sand bags at various points around the bay—pathetic little forts and outposts. "These islanders are hardy folk," observed Higgs, still struggling to keep spirits up. "They will defend hearth and home bravely."

Thompson lit up, exhaled, and frowned. "If the Germans put ashore a heavily armed landing party these hardy folk will all get slaughtered," said Number One in a sardonic monotone.

This remark took Higgs aback. However, he quickly realized that Thompson was right. "If I were Admiralty," he said after a tense moment of silence, "I'd keep *Canopus* here to help prevent a bloodbath. She's an albatross around our necks, but carries the big guns, smaller ordnance, and the Royal Marines these people need."

Thompson stared at Higgs a while, a look of incredulity on his face. "After Coronel I wouldn't count on too much rationality from Admiralty." He exhaled smoke again. "But, for what it's worth, I agree."

•   •   •

The two went ashore to conduct their business. Thompson hurried to Sapper Hill, the high ground south of town where workers constructed an observation post. Its tower provided a vantage point to see the East Asiatic Squadron if it took the same route the British ships had just used—the only way to approach Port Stanley from the south. Luce accompanied Higgs to Government House in order to give Allardyce an official report on the battle. The ships began the hapless, all-day task of taking on coal from colliers waiting there for this purpose. Other officers and petty officers not needed for coaling also went ashore for brief visits with their "up home" people—if they could be found.

After he finished with the dispatches, Higgs asked for, and received permission to visit his away-from-home family, the Hagas, as long as he returned to the ship well before her evening departure.

•   •   •

Higgs knocked at the door. Anne Mari opened it, staring incredulously at first, a deer-in-the-headlights look that quickly changed to one of excited surprise and anxiety-ending relief. "Thank God you're alive!" she cried, spreading her arms to offer a good friend a hug—that was immediately taken.

"I don't have much time," he said seriously, "but I had to make sure that my favorite Kelpers were safe and sound." As she grasped his hand and walked him into the living room, Higgs said, looking around, an even more worried look coming over him: "Where is everybody?"

"They say the German Army has executed thousands of innocent men, women, and children in Belgium and France. Beautiful Louvain and other whole cities have been razed to the ground. So London ordered the governor to evacuate everyone except those who are able to help defend the town."

"And your parents?"

"With his years at sea, Papa volunteered to be one of the lookouts on Sapper Hill. Mama and I and some of the other women will assist the town doctors as nurses. A military surgeon would certainly be welcome if one is available."

After the casualties of Coronel, the image of Falkland Islanders with wounds serious enough to require a military surgeon was about all Higgs could take. He sat down on the couch and buried head in hands.

What could he say? Thompson was right: a successful defense against German marines had no chance—but if civilians were to be lined up and shot anyway, what was the alternative but to fight? *Canopus* and her crew would definitely even the odds, but she too had been ordered to depart after coaling—it would be wrong, and cruel, to even raise the possibility of assistance from this ship, or any other ship for that matter. So Higgs said nothing.

Because his body language suggested the need to forget asking about a navy surgeon, Anne Mari got Aquavit and one glass from the cabinet and poured a modest portion. What would have seemed inappropriate and unacceptable to her in the peacetime of another year she did not question in the wartime of this one: Lloyd needed a drink.

"Talk to me, Lloyd. I know you are deeply troubled after what you've been through. But talk to me, talk it out. It helps, believe me."

He raised his head from his hands, but still said nothing for a moment. "Wouldn't that be rather selfish of me?" he said eventually, voice nearly breaking. "Brave Kelpers prepare to fight, and we who have fought and lost cry in our schnapps?"

"Please, tell me what troubles you ... please."

Higgs looked at her for a long time before his expression slowly yielded to her. But still he did not speak. And then finally he spilled his feelings.

"It's just this, Anne Mari. Britain is proud of the Royal Navy. For centuries the public has held us in such high esteem, such trust, such affection.[15] And how did we respond to that grave responsibility? In the first major naval engagement of the war the Imperial Navy of upstart Germany beat us—not just beat us, but almost annihilated us, and in a few minutes, without as far as could be seen inflicting any damage whatsoever on the enemy. We were humiliated to the very depths

---

15   From Hickling, *Sailor at Sea*. See my methodological Afterword.

213

of our beings. We feel bitterly ashamed of ourselves because we let down the king, we let down the Admiralty, and we let down England!"

"Lloyd, it just seems that way to you. No one here feels that way, and I'm sure no one in England does either. I haven't read a lot of history, but enough to know that you lost a battle, not the war. The Royal Navy has not given up, and nor will you."

"Yes, quite right that. But in the meantime, while England readies her revenge, our navy comrades will look at the officers and crew of *Glasgow* and, without saying it, but it'll be in their eyes, they'll question our bravery—why did we get away and not the others? Did the others do the fighting while we cut and ran?"

Anne Mari started to reply, but Higgs stopped her. "What is worse, why am I here and sixteen hundred others—my friends and all of those boys—at the bottom of the Pacific Ocean? Cradock wanted me to transfer to *Good Hope* but there was no opportunity before the battle. You see, I'm not just ashamed—I feel guilty. I *am* guilty."

"Listen to me Lloyd." He turned away. "No, look at me. There's no reason why these kinds of things happen. They just do in war. And it surely has nothing to do with your courage or the courage of every man on His Majesty's Ship *Glasgow*. The Royal Navy will come back to this island—we all know this—and when it does, your friends here, and your comrades in the Royal Navy, will welcome *Glasgow* into their battle line. Of these things I am certain."

Her words seemed to make Higgs feel a little better. Eventually he nodded and said: "Well, I suppose you're right. At least I hope you are ... but I really must go. The ships will be leaving tonight."

"Oh please stay a while—Mama and Papa will be returning soon. It will give them heart to see you. Please stay." She pointed to the bottle teasingly. After a brief moment, they both burst out in laughter, which, even more than talking, is the best release.

The gravity of the military moment had not passed, not by a long stretch, but Lloyd Higgs did feel better. In part it was the Aquavit and in part the talking, the laughing, and the socializing—he stayed for a full two hours to spend time with Mathilda and Carl Anton. Higgs also felt better after he procured a 55-gallon barrel of beer from the "Rose and Crown." Weightier by far, however, was the realization that he had feelings for Anne Mari that went beyond friendship—and he was fairly certain that she felt the same.

* * *

The Royal Navy did indeed return to Port Stanley—and much sooner than anyone thought possible. While approaching Montevideo on November 10th, *Canopus* once again had to reduce speed because of trouble in the engine room. When this news was wired ahead to Admiral Stoddart, who relayed it to London, Fisher advised a distraught Churchill that *Canopus* should return to the Falklands. Her contingent of Royal Marines meant a backbone-steadying reinforcement of the island's volunteers. Dismantled, her ten 6-inch guns would significantly bolster the island's beach defenses.

Fisher wanted the ship itself grounded at the far eastern edge of the harbor behind the dunes of Hooker's Point, where her four 12-inch rifles guarded both the wireless station and the approaches to Port William.

Churchill understood irony as well as anyone: *Canopus* was finally a citadel.

XXI
INTO THE
SOUTH ATLANTIC

The fortification of Port Stanley actually came last in a frenetic series of moves Admiralty made to catch and destroy Graf Spee. Tirpitz claimed in his memoirs that the British had to wipe away the humiliation of Coronel if they were to reestablish the prestige of the Royal Navy so vital to the empire's survival. He also pointed to the world of neutral nations waiting, for the moment, to see if Great Britain could retain her modern day supremacy at sea now that the era of wind and sail had passed. Tirpitz's memoirs bristle with exaggerations and distortions, but these statements, at least, were smack-on accurate.

Churchill and Fisher caucused in the War Room on November 9th, the day of *Emden*'s demise, to finalize their plans for sinking the rest of the East Asiatic Squadron. The First Lord had received panicky telegrams from Admiral David Beatty, commander of the battle cruiser squadron at Cromarty Firth, and Admiral John Jellicoe, commander of the main concentration of dreadnought battleships at Scapa Flow, protesting Churchill's decision to send two battle cruisers into the South Atlantic with Mountbatten's former chief of staff, Admiral Sturdee, and a third battle cruiser into the Caribbean.

. . .

"Jellicoe and Beatty are shitting bricks," said the First Lord with a wry smile as he looked over the missives from Beatty and Jellicoe. "Should the German High Seas Fleet come out, our need for the missing three battle cruisers will be bitterly felt," writes Beatty. Jellicoe goes further: "I hope I won't be held responsible if the fleet's force is unequal to the task devolving upon it."

"You know, Fisher," Churchill continued, "We *have* pretty much stripped Beatty clean."

"Let them shit their bricks," barked Fisher. "It's not about whether we have five battle cruisers or two against the Germans—that's rot—it's about gunnery."

Churchill looked perplexed by the final statement. "Their gunnery was pretty damned good at Coronel, Fisher."

"Ours will be better," said the First Sea Lord confidently, "but you're making a mistake by giving the South Atlantic command to Sturdee."

Fisher's tactlessness, normally limitless, now came close to its outer reaches. "Sturdee *is, has been, and always will be* a pedantic ass! Never has there been such rot as that perpetrated by him in his world-wide dispersal of weak units before the Battle of Coronel. The problem up to now was that he apportioned tortoises to catch Von Spee's hares, and a million tortoises can't catch a hare. The Almighty created greyhounds to catch hares, and this is what we're going to do."

Churchill turned a little red in the face at hearing this because he, after all, had approved the disastrous 'world-wide dispersal of weak units.' Nevertheless, he had to defend his selection.

"You underestimate Sturdee," said the First Lord sternly. "He was the first to suggest sending battle cruisers, and we overruled him."

"He says that *now*," said Fisher with Olympian distain. "You'll regret this appointment ... But enough of this. Let me show you our concentrations against the East Asiatic."

He continued, using a pointer to demonstrate his concentrations. "Intelligence places the German squadron steaming west out of Valparaiso. We do not know where it is now, or where it's heading, but as you can see we are assembling five powerful squadrons, and the Japanese are providing two more, to stop Von Spee wherever he decides to sail."

"If he goes back into the Pacific the Japanese can block him with battleships and heavy cruisers *here*, in the Carolines, and *here*, at Suva."

"If he escapes up the west coast of South America a squadron can stop him that is forming *here*, in the Galapagos Islands. Battle cruiser *Australia* has been dispatched to join them. And if he eludes that battle group and slips through the Canal we presently have the 13.5-inch guns of battle cruiser *Princess Royal* and other supporting vessels *here*, in the Western Caribbean."

"If he rounds Cape Horn and crosses the South Atlantic we have him outgunned with *Defence* and *Minotaur* when they arrive *here*, in Cape Town."

"If he moves *here*, up the coast of Argentina, which is what I predict he'll do, we are reinforcing Stoddart's now-marginal flotilla with battle cruisers *Invincible* and *Inflexible*."

"And if he eludes these two greyhounds and slips up the Atlantic toward Europe, we are concentrating a superior squadron *here*, in Cape Verde. Flanking the old battleship *Vengeance* we have armored cruisers *Warrior* and *Black Prince*, nearly equal in armament to *Minotaur* and *Defence*. We destroy Von Spee whatever he decides."

Listening to this, Churchill kept nodding his approval, but skepticism in his eyes trumped the more positive body language.

"To achieve the destruction of five German ships, by my count, Fisher, we are employing thirty British. This includes four battle cruisers and four big armored cruisers. We can't totally ignore the concerns of Jellicoe and Beatty. The German fleet may come out to break the blockade, especially if they know our numbers are down so dangerously close to theirs. We *must* do the job quickly."

The First Lord paused. "The South Atlantic worries me. If Von Spee hurries, and goes where you think he will, he'll seize Port Stanley, disrupt trade off Argentina, overpower Stoddart, and then disappear long before your two greyhounds can get there. He could easily slip past the Cape Verde squadron too. Britain, which has long ruled the waves, will look like a laughable, helpless cork bobbing on the sea."

He stopped to pull a telegram from his coat. "The Admiralty Superintendent, Devonport, reports that the earliest possible date for installing the new fire control system, completing the dry dock repairs, and full provisioning of *Invincible* and *Inflexible* is midnight 13th November. Shall I give him a prog?"

Fisher took the telegram, read it, and then blurted: "Friday the 13th! What a day to choose!"

"Okay then, I'll order him to have the ships at sea on the 11th come what may. There's no time to lose."

•   •   •

While Graf Spee idled away four more days on Más Afuera, the two big fast ships left Devonport and steamed away to Cape Verde, Vice-Admiral Frederick Doveton Sturdee commanding, with orders to assume operational control of the South Atlantic once he got there. Fifty-five years old, Graf Spee's new adversary had a decent if not stellar reputation in the Royal Navy. He knew naval tactics well, seemed immune to the pressure of any situation, sometimes to the point of obliviousness, and had demonstrated a praiseworthy loyalty to superiors as he rose prudently through the ranks. The haughty First Sea Lord never forgave Sturdee, in fact, for showing more loyalty to his own commander in the Mediterranean than Fisher in London, which largely explains the outburst against Churchill's choice of the man to track down and destroy Graf Spee.

Fisher had sensed something correctly about Sturdee, however—an ominous, intuitive feeling that this man was *not* right for the job. Indeed, the Royal Navy's avenger seemed strangely, foggily ill-attuned to the urgency of his mission. His ship's turbines could have sped reinforcement south at 26-28 knots, but he crept at 10 knots to conserve fuel and rest the stokers, not reaching Cape Verde until November 18th. Britain, however, lacked neither coal nor coaling places, and why rest the stokers thousands of miles from any potential battle? After setting sail again on the 19th Sturdee paused for much-needed target practice, moreover, but at only 6,000-12,000 yards rather than 16,000-to-18,000 yards, where he possessed a decisive advantage against Spee's armored cruisers. He also veered away from mission course to search for *Karlsruhe*, which, if anyone's domain, assignment, and priority, was *Princess Royal*'s, not his.

Finally, on November 26th, Sturdee joined Stoddart's ships at Abrolhos Rocks, 250 miles north of Rio de Janeiro. This collection of low-lying reefs provided scant protection from trade winds and ocean swells and thus was less than ideal for coaling, but because the Rocks lay just outside Brazilian waters the Royal Navy used this site frequently. Stoddart had brought the squadron he would have been forced to use against Graf Spee if the Germans had sailed for Cape Horn right after Coronel: two up-to-date light cruisers, *Glasgow* and *Bristol*; three obsolete armored cruisers, *Kent*, *Cornwall*, and *Carnavon*, and the more impressive *Defence* with her broadside of four 9.2-inch and five 7.5-inch rifles. The imposing armored cruiser would now sail for South Africa to join her sister, *Minotaur*.

Frederick Sturdee: "Very well, Luce, we'll sail tomorrow"
(Imperial War Museum)

By this point twenty-two days had passed since the East Asiatic Squadron steamed out of Valparaiso on November 4th. If it had headed that day for the Horn, not Más Afuera, a major clash off Montevideo in mid-November loomed. That London did not like its chances in a Stoddart vs. Spee match up after Coronel's frightening demonstration of "pretty damn good" German gunnery, opting instead to "rush" battle cruisers south, is one way to demonstrate that Graf Spee had exaggerated the hopelessness of his situation. By concentrating the combined broadsides of his armored cruisers' twelve 8.2-inch and six 5.9-inch guns against *Defence*—eighteen rifles that could do damage at 12,000 yards versus only nine—and sinking the enemy flagship, Spee would have forced Stoddart's older vessels to disengage before they got into range. Or, if they chose to engage, Spee could have outrun them to preserve shells, coaling in Pernambuco, 2,100 miles farther north, and slipping into the vast, relatively defenseless Central Atlantic on a northwesterly course for the Caribbean well before Sturdee neared South American waters at tortoise pace. It is tempting to speculate, in other words, that if Graf Spee had departed right away for the South Atlantic, even at a slow pace to preserve coal, rather than succumbing to fatalistic inaction, his pursuers would have required very good luck to prevent him from reaching the North Atlantic, the last leg of a remarkable cruise, and a chance to turn the nightmares of Beatty and Jellicoe into reality.

•   •   •

On the morning of November 27th, Sturdee convened his captains aboard the flagship, *Invincible*, to discuss his plans. Captain Luce of *Glasgow* returned from the meeting greatly disturbed. He sent for Thompson and Higgs and spread out a chart of the South Atlantic on his cabin table.

"Admiralty has finally sent word of Von Spee's whereabouts. Our agents placed him *here*, in the Gulf of Penas, on the 21st. Even though that was six days ago, Sturdee still intends to coal and provision for two more days, depart on the 29th for Port Stanley, 2,200 miles away, coal again there, and then slip around the Horn, supposedly before the Germans do. I said I thought he underestimated the threat to Port Stanley and that the Germans could already be closing in on it if they weighed anchor four or five days ago. So we agreed, as a precaution, that Governor Allardyce send a daily wireless signal—no signal means that Spee has gotten there first. How do you two see things?"

"Sturdee seems out of touch with reality," said Thompson. "Surely Admiralty has ordered him to get the lead out."

Higgs added: "Sir, he *does* take the threat to the Falklands too lightly. I fear for the volunteers and especially for the civilians. We all know what the Huns did in Belgium!"

"Exactly, quite right," stated Luce boldly to Higgs. Turning to Thompson, he had already decided what to do: "Number One, I am rather exercised about this delay. I think I'll go back over and try and persuade the admiral to sail earlier."

• • •

Within the hour Luce sat at a large mahogany table in Sturdee's spacious day cabin. "What's on your mind, Luce?" said the admiral.

"I hope you don't mind me coming over, sir, and please don't imagine I am questioning your orders, but thinking it over I feel we should sail earlier."

"But dammit, Luce, we're sailing the day after tomorrow, isn't that soon enough for you? Anyhow, why didn't you raise the point at the conference earlier today?"

"Perhaps, sir, I was at fault. I didn't make myself clear enough as to the situation ashore at Stanley. Allardyce is very worried and thinks the Germans may invade any time, and I agree with him. When I left Stanley with *Canopus* he felt that the navy was abandoning the islanders to their fate."

"*Canopus* is there now, Luce—she's gone back."

"Yes, sir, but she's immobilized. She can't help much if the Germans land out of range of her guns. As for the Falkland Island Volunteers, they're mostly a bunch of sheppards, and even with the help of Royal Marines they'll be of little use against landing parties covered by the guns of *Scharnhorst* and *Gneisenau*."

"Don't you think Allardyce knows that we're coming to his rescue?"

"No, sir. In the interests of security I imagine he's not been told."

Sturdee stood up and paced around for a moment. Somewhat reluctantly he changed plans: "Very well, Luce, we'll sail tomorrow."

At 1000 hours on Saturday, November 28th, Sturdee's ships left Abrolhos Rocks. On December 3rd while still a day out of Montevideo, Higgs received two wireless messages and rushed them to Luce.

"Sir, four days ago our people spotted the German squadron off the western end of the Magellan Straits only a hundred miles from the cape. And just yesterday German colliers left Montevideo on a southerly course. Von Spee must be planning a rendezvous soon. He must already be around the Horn!"

XXII
CAPE HORN

At 1600 hours, November 15th, the East Asiatic Squadron left gloomy Más Afuera, steaming southeastward toward a new and uncertain destiny. That day, a depressing Sunday, brought tears to our eyes, for every ship's chaplain had asked us to pray for the families of our brave mates on the *Emden*, whose dreadful fate we had learned about two days earlier. We also mourned the loss of Tsingtao, our home-away-from-home, taken by the Japanese at about the same time, and the deaths of comrades there who had defended our colony to the last. Neither piece of bad, psyche-piercing news did anything to raise an already sagging morale.

As we progressed to the south the weather became increasingly cold and bad.[16] On the evening of November 20th we turned landwards and entered the Gulf of Penas at daybreak. Gradually rocks emerged from a curtain of fog.

What a different scene from those we knew in the tropics! Here we found not lively, steamy jungles and white sand beaches, but rather silent, frozen forests,

16   From Pochhammer, *Before Jutland*. See my methodological Afterword.

rocks, mountains, and glaciers. One of these giant sheets of ice stretched right down to the sea, and as the sun rose higher and shot its beams down, the glacier came alit, all its crevasses and moraines easily distinguishable. We saw no living thing around. Cool air, easily breathed, filled our lungs and rendered work less wearisome. It was not for pleasure, after all, that we had ventured into this dangerous channel. Indeed we had work to do—coaling, of course.

We had a long cruise before us. Three of our colliers, emptied of their valuable cargo, would soon depart, leaving us only three half-full steamers. Graf Spee had arranged a rendezvous with additional colliers off the Argentine coast, but coaling at sea would be impossible in waters likely to be stormy and nobody could say for sure what would happen on the other side of South America, so we coaled like never before. When we got the bunkers full to the brim, coal was piled up on deck to great heights. Both sides of the middle deck were stacked so high that it sagged and had to be supported from below. Between the third and fourth funnels there remained only enough room for our steam launch.

The enemy was somewhere on the vast ocean, and he would, without a doubt, want to settle accounts for our victory at Coronel—or his name was not England. The only option that remained to us was to slip through to the Atlantic, where hopefully we were not yet expected, and hopefully help waited. Maerker told me that the admiral received encouraging word after we dropped anchors. Our naval agent in San Francisco had requested a battle cruiser to reinforce us. Would Admiralty comply? Did this mean that after long delays *Moltke* had put to sea to help us? No one held out great hope, but maybe—just maybe—she would join us after we rounded Cape Horn!

Our thoughts veered towards the north, in the direction of home. With or without help, if only we could force our way through, and, even with battered ships and torn flags, clasp again the hands of our brothers in the Fatherland! Christmas was not far off—who could say where we would be at Christmas—with our loved ones?

Because colliers were being detached that could take letters home to families we could not be certain we would ever see again, Graf Spee encouraged all ships' companies to use what might be the last opportunity to communicate with loved ones. Of course he did not use these words, but the officers and, I suspect, most of the men, knew what he meant.

• • •

Pochhammer was right. Most crewmen of the East Asiatic took advantage of this opportunity. For many of the officers and old hands, nightmarish worries about their ultimate fate had become increasingly difficult to shake off. All men of the sea knew about its natural dangers, but navy men harbored an even deeper anxiety about the man-made catastrophe that might befall them.

Not all of the German sailors perceived themselves in perilous circumstances, however, or at least they had fooled themselves into feeling that their chances were good. Such an upbeat way of looking at things is fairly common among combatants—it is a kind of psychological survival mechanism.

But sometimes sailors and soldiers are just naïve. Something more like this explained the thinking of Johannes Bauer as he, too, wrote a letter:

"At Sea   *November 23rd 1914*
The weeks since our goodbyes, my dearest Simone, seem like years. I trust that you and your father are well. Hopefully the war has imposed no particular hardships on you or anyone else in Valparaiso.

As for me, I am well. It is good to be back at sea even though life aboard ship, especially the never-ending task of loading coal into bunkers, is especially strenuous and dirty. I sometimes wonder whether I shall ever be clean again! Anyway, it is good to know that I am serving the Fatherland and not shirking duty in swanky civilian clothes.

As for what this duty will be, what our mission is, I don't know—and couldn't say even if I did. All of the men speculate endlessly, but I sometimes get the impression that most of the officers don't know either. I suspect that our mission will be what I said it would be that last sacred day we spent together on the heights over the roadstead. Whatever our mission, however, and whatever our destiny, know that I love you and yearn for the day—which will come!!—when my duty is done and we can begin our married life."

Given Simone's apprehensive mood on the day of Johannes' departure, it is doubtful that this letter reassured her. At any rate, the young petty officer soon found himself face to face with the stark reality of his situation—and it was not very reassuring. One day in the Gulf of Penas, while his torpedo crew went about its daily routine, he made a bold assertion.

"My money's on us using this remote bay as a base to shut down English trade with Chile. See how they like trying to make explosives without Chile's nitrate ores."

"I don't know about that," said a second sailor. "Word on some of the coal ships is they're takin' off. The admiral wouldn't do that if he's stayin' here, now would he? He's stackin' coal high for a long voyage. I'm bettin' he's roundin' the Horn."

"Well, that makes sense, I guess," replied Bauer. "Commerce raiding will be just as effective off Argentina. Everyone says a long war is economically impossible. So destroying commerce brings even quicker victory for the Fatherland."

The young man had quickly become well-liked by his shipmates, but his higher social status kept a certain distance between him and most of the crew. He was also not regular navy. Both factors contributed to some of them delighting a little too much in one-upping him. But, in fact, there was one possibility for the squadron that he had not consciously considered.

"He's not roundin' the Horn to capture steamers, Bauer," said a third man. "One of the stewards in the officers' mess swears he heard them talking about making it all the way back to Germany to do battle with the English. Our admiral wants to win the war that way, not by sinking merchant ships. Bet on it, Bauer, bet on it!"

When Bauer heard this, a rather startled look came over his face like a sudden weather break at sea. He looked as if he pondered for the very first time what he had gotten himself into. After a moment, however, he mustered some self-composure, at least on the outside.

"That's fine with me," he said, masking his inner anxiety. "I *will* bet on it. Woe to any English who get in *our* way. My money's on *us*!"

• • •

On the afternoon of November 26[17] we once again put to sea and got caught up almost immediately in the swell of a heavy southwesterly sea.[17] A proper Cape Horn wind blew in our faces. Ropes were extended all over the ship so that men could keep their balance. The boats and other heavy objects were double lashed to prevent them from breaking away. Doors and portholes were firmly shut, but despite this water leaked everywhere, such that the air on the ship became cold and humid. The heavy cruisers stood up to the storm well, but the light cruisers, which had also stacked huge mounds of coal on deck, began to roll violently. We could see the waves going over them and their bows shipping water. Eventually they had to heave to and throw most of their deck coal overboard lest they capsize—ominous bad luck!

The farther south we proceeded, the worse the weather became. The first evening out we could still

---

17   From Pochhammer, *Before Jutland*. See my methodological Afterword.

take our meals in the ward room comfortably on tables rolling with the waves, but beginning on November 27th keeping plates and glasses steady on the tables was out of the question. We had to stretch ropes across the room. Each man took a plate, stumbled across to the buffet table, received a portion of food, and squatted in some corner, trying with plate and glass to adapt himself to the pitching and rolling of the ship. After a few days of this most of the crockery was broken. Sometimes this was a source of great amusement.

But morale was essentially poor—and getting poorer. As we plied ever closer to Cape Horn, thoughts about life and thoughts about death entered our minds. Some of us had lived longer than others, some of us had accomplished more than others, but, regardless, how long would we continue to live? How much longer would we breathe this fresh cold air? When would the end come? In Germany, as old men, many years later surrounded by grandchildren? Or perhaps soon, under 30-foot waves like those crashing over our bows? When we closed our eyes for the last time, would our position at sea be nameless, our fate unknown? Would Germany hear only that we had vanished, that we were missing? Would we have no last word of farewell to those nearest to us, whose love and fidelity winged their emotional way to us from the other side of the world? Would the end come quickly, or would it be slow, gruesome, and torturing?

I ask you: who among those who have fought for hearth and home has not harbored such fearful thoughts? I remember that we often spoke of these things quite openly and naturally as November 1914 drew to a close. To be ready for anything, to follow the orders of our admiral, and if it came to it, if we fired our guns again and got into a hotter battle, to do our duty to the best of our ability—more than this we could not do. More than this no soldier or sailor can do.

Slowly but steadily, creeping along at only five knots, making at most fifty miles a day against the sea, we worked our way south. On November 29th we passed the opening to the Straits of Magellan. After this we altered course to the southeast, and the weather finally improved. On December 2nd, while rocking on a gentle after swell, we sighted, far ahead and off to port, the southern promontory of the American continent. "Well, so this is your famous Cape Horn," said one of the men.

While we rendered to this inhospitable strand of land the homage that was due it, a huge iceberg, colored pale blue by the sun's rays, appeared off the starboard bow. It was 70 yards high and 650 yards long. "Iceberg in sight" was shouted all over the ship, and the men were allowed to come on deck to see it pass.

The thought that we might collide with it at night or in a fog caused us some uneasiness, but it was extinguished in the shouts of laughter that arose when one sailor, our young banker from Valparaiso, made a hilarious suggestion. "Lads, lets make fast to its port side—for coaling!" Where do we get such volunteers, good German men so willing to laugh at adversity?

"Sail ship six points to port," shouted the lookout in the crow's nest of the *Gneisenau*, and from our station on the bridge we now saw a three-master tacking nearer to land. *Leipzig* left the line to inspect, and soon after came the call: "English ship, English cargo, 2,800 tons of coal." We could not let this rich prize escape us, especially after the light cruisers had lost so much coal in the storms that they did not have enough left to reach Argentina. We took it into our line.

On a fine clear night of the southern summer we entered Beagle Channel, named after Charles Darwin's famous ship. We disturbed a pack of seals that quickly dived off the rocks on which they basked, and on December 3rd, at 0500 hours, we anchored off the east coast of Picton Island in about twenty-eight fathoms of water. We should have made it to this anchorage on November 30th—the storms had delayed our progress a good three days.

Later that day the coaling process began anew. This would add another three days to our cruise. A few of the junior officers felt these delays would seal our fate, that the English would now have time to send ships to block our way. Some even argued that this sailing ship was an enemy trap planted here to slow us down. The prevailing sentiment in the ward room, however, had turned optimistic—after all, we had the excruciating voyage around the Cape behind us. It was no longer time for seeing black, for hanging crepe.

•   •   •

Maybe Pochhammer and the optimists were fooling themselves? At any rate, with coaling nearly complete at 0800 hours on December 6th, Graf Spee assembled all captains in his conference suite. The admiral had decided to seize Port Stanley, which intelligence sources reported free of British warships, and take its governor hostage. He wanted to retaliate for the capture of German Samoa and arrest of its governor, deprive Britain of an important wireless station and its only good harbor in the region, as well as give Germany a bargaining chip at any future peace conference. Finally, and most importantly, Graf Spee believed he could strike another major blow to the prestige of Britain and make an impression on neutral fence-sitting nations.

German steamers rushed south to Puerto Santa Elena, southern Argentina, with 10,000 tons of coal as well as cement, entrenching tools, barbed wire, and other supplies for the fortification of Port Stanley. Squadron marines, reinforced by German émigré volunteers from across South America, would be asked to hold the port. After the seizure of Port Stanley and coaling at Puerto Santa Elena, Graf Spee intended to sail to Pernambuco, Brazil, coal again, and then break for the North Atlantic.

This plan found the support of Spee's chief of staff, Fielitz, his second, Pfahl, and Captain Schönberg of *Nürnberg*. Schultz, Maerker, and the other two light cruiser captains thought it wiser to circumvent Port Stanley, where British warships likely waited, and descend on the British shipping lanes off the River Platte.

The admiral, of course, had never been particularly interested in commerce raiding. More to the point, after Valparaiso the squadron's psychically-tortured leader had not shaken off an ever more deeply entrenched despondency regarding the squadron's chances. His nature would not let him. So it made scant difference to Graf Spee whether the Royal Navy waited for them in Port Stanley, the Caribbean, or the English Channel—they probably would not make it back anyway. Even if a battle cruiser joined them—a remote possibility—that was a far cry from two dreadnoughts. The man in him struggled to ensure that they rationally maximize their chances of survival in the service of the Fatherland, but the fatalist in him constantly got in the way—hence his plan to raid Port Stanley.

．　．　．

"The River Platte is the last place I want to go," objected Graf Spee somewhat meekly. "The information I have places armored cruisers *Defence*, *Carnavon*, and *Cornwall* there—perhaps *Canopus* too. We have to avoid another pitched battle with magazines half-empty until we get nearer to the home fleet," he said with some authority but little conviction.

Not surprisingly, Maerker remained unconvinced. "Might we discuss your intelligence sources? How reliable are they? How recent is this information?"

Although not happy about having to explain—it was natural to feel this way, for explaining is losing—Spee rather indifferently obliged his old friend. "The telegram from the German consul in Montevideo reached me in the Gulf of Penas two weeks ago. As for no warships in Port Stanley, I also have a telegram dated November 15th from the German consul in Punta Arenas, just around Cape Horn. The captain of a British steamer was overheard saying that there were no warships at Port Stanley, his previous port of call."

"Leaving aside the real possibility that an empty Port Stanley is simply disinformation put out by British Intelligence," said Maerker, "just let me say that so much could have changed in two weeks, not to mention four. That British steamer must have left Port Stanley on November 10th or 11th. If Port Stanley is important enough for us to seize and hold, the British will be similarly motivated to defend it. They have had ample time to send warships there from the Platte. I urge you to reconsider this plan. I recommend that we coal at Puerto Santa Elena, move on to Pernambuco, and then disappear into the vastness of the Atlantic."

Maerker paused to formulate a final thought: "Even if the British ships are still off the Platte, and they have nothing to defend Port Stanley, our taking it will expend too much ammunition—and, as you said, we have to preserve shells for the final dash through the British blockade." He gathered his thoughts. "What is more important: taking Port Stanley—or getting home and winning the war?"

For a long time Spee mulled over this advice, walking over to the map, studying it, and pacing back and forth. For those in the room it was an excruciating delay. The thought process was also very painful for him: fight for the Fatherland today, or play it safe, disappear, and survive—but only to fight and die another day. Did it make much difference? It did, said one voice, *but did it really*, asked another?

Finally the Count walked back to the others. He seemed more tired than usual and not especially committed to the righteousness of his decision. "I agree that it's a risk, but it's a risk I'm willing to take. We must seize every opportunity to help the Fatherland in its hour of need—and to hurt the enemy in his. If Britain loses a colony, the whole world of neutral nations will doubt her power. Gentlemen, thank you for your comments. We sail for the Falklands today, 1200 hours."

XXIII
PORT STANLEY

Carl Anton Haga and one of his senior Norwegian employees had volunteered for the Island Defense Force and been assigned to the tower on Sapper Hill for the morning watch. By 0900 on Monday, December 7th, the two Scandinavians had been scanning the seas through binoculars and taking turns at their more powerful telescope for a few hours, one looking south, the other east.

Even though it was a stormy day like so many lately that obscured vision, suddenly Haga saw smoke clouds a good fifteen miles to sea off the entrance to Port William. Both men looked at the approaching smudges for a moment until a wind shift enabled them to see something through the smoke. "Five warships, maybe more!" exclaimed Haga. He picked up the phone and sounded the alarm.

Within minutes, word spread through the town in a chain reaction of anxiety and terror. Taking his morning walk, Governor Allardyce was full of worries about the safety of his people, who some weeks earlier had all returned to town from their evacuation areas. As he neared the Anglican Cathedral a commotion in front of it jerked him out of his silent deliberations. A throng

241

of people charged at him, shouting and frantically waving their arms.

The lead man ran right up to the governor, almost knocking him down. "They've come, sir, they're in sight from Sapper Hill!"

Allardyce, turning pale, quickly asked: "Who, the Germans?"

"No, sir, they say it's our own ships! Sir, we're saved!"

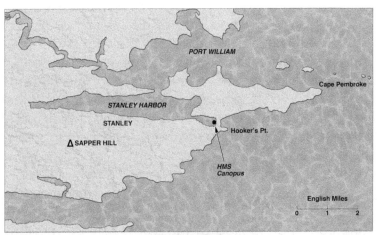

PORT STANLEY
(Peter Groesbeck)

"How many," inquired Allardyce, noticeably relieved.

"They've counted eight so far and there are two big ones with three-leg masts!"

Allardyce walked up the steep Sapper Hill, mounted the tower, and asked Haga for the telescope. Coming just into focus, a pack of ships, all flying the Union Jack, approached Port William. He turned to Haga. "Carl, thanks to God for our deliverance! This is a personal intervention by the Almighty!"

The three men stood on top of the tower for the next hour, watching as *Glasgow* and *Bristol* entered the inner harbor, the rest of the squadron anchoring outside in the roadstead. Two colliers inched alongside the light cruisers to begin the inevitable refueling process. Apparently the big battle cruisers would have to wait their turn so that one of these faster vessels could commence patrolling nearby waters. Thus far, however, neither light cruiser captain had received orders to put out.

·   ·   ·

That afternoon Admiral Sturdee convened all squadron captains and top-ranking officers in his suite to discuss operations. Like many of the other officers, Luce, Thompson, and Higgs worried about squadron coaling that would stretch well into the next day, for ships remained vulnerable while dead in the water taking on fuel, but at least the Royal Navy had arrived in time to protect their beloved islanders. Their unease mounted, however, when Sturdee asserted that Von Spee still cruised off the coast of Chile, when surely, it seemed to them, he must be either anchored in a coastal haven somewhere near Cape Horn, slipping into the South Atlantic and eluding the battle cruisers sent to destroy him, or—in the worst case scenario—heading straight for Port Stanley.

With the meeting over and the officers filing out and up to the quarterdeck, Sturdee, who was seeing them over the side, approached Captain Heathcote Salusbury Grant of *Canopus*. "Oh Grant, come back to my cabin, I want to hear what you have done."

243

They went back down. Grant unfolded a gridded chart. "I thought you might be interested, sir, so I brought this over." He spread it out, and together they placed paper weights on the four corners.

"Here's *Canopus*. We opened the sea cocks and settled her down in shallow water right behind the wireless station. Masts and funnels were removed so that she is totally obscured from view by sea. She's blind to sea too, but here are the observation posts to control indirect fire. The approaches to the island and all of Port William are thus covered up to the maximum range of her four 12-inch guns, say twelve-to-thirteen thousand yards. We landed our 6-inch guns here, to cover the beaches against landing parties."

"Splendid Grant. Have you fired the guns?"

"Yes sir, we did a calibration, and considering the age of the guns, the results were surprisingly accurate."

"What about putting on a practice shoot tomorrow?"

"Certainly, sir. It will of course be with reduced charges and blank projectiles to save wear and tear on the guns. I'll have the gun crews ready the magazines and handling rooms with the practice charges and shells before sunset so that we're ready for you first thing tomorrow."

"Good, Grant. Shall we say at 0900?"

It was agreed, and Grant left to prepare his ship for a harmless, impotent target shoot.

• • •

At 2300 hours, German time, December 7th, shortly after Sturdee dismissed Grant, Margarete, *Graefin* von

Spee, went through her usual bedtime ritual. Her beautiful, gracefully aging Germanic features covered up an uneasiness churning inside her. Sitting at a mirrored cosmetics table, she applied moisturizer to her face, let down her hair, and combed it out thoroughly. Once finished, she walked to a bedside nightstand, picked up a small, golden, cylindrical calendar, and turned a knob on the side to set the date for the next day such that it now read December 8th.

The countess soon fell sound asleep. At 0300 as a large wall piece chimed three times, however, her peaceful countenance became more and more disturbed. At last Margarete woke up with a start and sat abruptly upright in bed. Sweating, her hair sticking to face and neck, she had a look of absolute horror. Finally she cried out and shook her head as if trying to banish a specter she had seen.

The countess was having a nightmare. She had had many of these in recent months—Graf Spee's attempts to prepare her for his death had been clumsy and insensitive, producing the opposite effect intended. What awoke her in such a terrible state of mind was a vision of her husband's ship, and her sons' ships, destroyed and burning, sinking beneath the waves.

In the Falklands clocks read 2100 hours the previous day, December 7th. The German squadron steamed north nearly twelve hours away from the entrance to Port William. So it must have been merely a nightmare—or maybe something else, perhaps a *premonition* of death at sea, of her entire family, dying, somewhere at sea?

The next day Margarete scanned the newspapers for stories about her husband's command. Finding nothing, she felt a little better. Apparently it had only been another nightmare.

• • •

At 1700 hours the next day, December 8th—noontime in the Falklands—the First Lord of the Admiralty worked at his office desk in the Admiralty Building. His chief of staff, Admiral Oliver, entered with a telegram from Captain Grant of *Canopus*.

Churchill opened it and read it aloud: "Admiral Spee arrived at daylight this morning with all his ships and is now in action with Admiral Sturdee's whole fleet, which was coaling."

Churchill looked at Oliver as if it were the worst moment of his life. A chill had gone up his spine. Finally he found some words: "Have we been taken by surprise and, in spite of all our superiority, mauled, unready, at anchor?! Can it mean that?!"

Oliver, himself clearly unnerved, said only: "I hope not."

Once, years after VE Day, Lord Cobham asked Churchill what were his most anxious moments during World War I and World War II. Without a hesitation, remarkably enough, the old war horse answered: "When they told me that Von Spee had surprised Sturdee in harbor at the Falkland Islands while *Invincible* and *Inflexible* were coaling."

• • •

At 0735 hours, Tuesday, December 8th, a sparkling clear morning for the first time in many days, Carl Anton Haga and his trusted employee once again stood atop their Sapper Hill perch. The whaling executive thought he saw smoke to the southeast, raised his binoculars, and alerted his fellow watcher. "You're right," said the other man after peering through the telescope: "Ships approaching."

Haga picked up his phone and rang up *Canopus*'s land fire control tower with the alarming news. A few minutes later, having studied the unfolding situation further, he phoned again: "Two men-of-war, one with four funnels, one with two, ten miles to sea steering northwards. Other ships farther out."

On board the island's "citadel," Grant paced the quarterdeck, waiting somewhat anxiously for the target shoot. A signalman rushed up to him: "Sir, gunnery officer ashore has just phoned through to say two German warships are approaching!"

Grant ordered immediately: "Run up flags: 'Enemy-in-Sight.' " He looked impatiently through binoculars to the center of Stanley Harbor to see if *Glasgow*, the nearest ship, had gotten the message.

A commotion already energized the early morning watch on board the light cruiser. Sapper Hill's signalman had alerted her too. Noticing the warning signal, officer of the watch Lieutenant Nigel Lyon roused the skipper from bed. Coming topside with a jacket over his pajamas, Lyon reported the news to Luce, who also ordered up flags for "Enemy-in-Sight" and to alert the flagship using signal lights.

Five minutes passed, however, and no word came from *Invincible*—shrouded in dust from coaling, she could see nothing. "Lyon, have you got that signal through to the flagship?"

"Not yet, sir, we've been trying for five minutes."

"Well, for God's sake do something about it—fire a gun, send a boat, don't just stand there like a stuffed dummy!"

Glasgow fired off her 3-inch saluting cannon, which woke up the crew below off watch and sent them scrambling topside. When Higgs appeared, Luce yelled to him: "Higgs, go to the masthead with the silhouette book and identify those ships. Sapper Hill says one has two funnels, but dammit, no German warship has two funnels!"

Higgs ascended the foremast as quickly as his half-asleep body could take him. It took him a few minutes, but after reaching the observation truck 150-feet up, catching his breath, and sighting the ships, he flipped hurriedly through his book and bellowed back down: "*Gneisenau* and *Nürnberg*—rest of German squadron farther out!"

The small cannon succeeded in getting the attention of the flagship. Sturdee had just showered and was shaving with a towel around his waste. The shot startled him, and he cut his cheek. Seconds later his flag lieutenant entered the bathroom: "Important signal from *Glasgow*, sir."

"What is it? Are we under fire?"

"No sir, at least not yet, sir: Sapper Hill lookouts report two ships in sight to the southward."

"Excuse me a minute, Flags." Sturdee closed the door, emerging half-dressed a minute later. "It's Von Spee all right, and here we are caught with half-empty bunkers—and to think he has walked straight to our doorstep. And *Canopus* is loaded with blanks. What rotten luck," he said, shaking his head. "Ask the Flag Captain and Engineer Commander to see me."

After a few minutes the two entered the cabin of the now fully uniformed admiral. "What a fix to be in," said Sturdee, not seeming to realize just yet what the real fix was. "If we go on coaling, the enemy may give us the slip, but if we stop we may not have enough coal to fight a running action."

Flag Captain Beamish and Commander Weeks, the chief engineering officer, looked at one another in astonishment. Finally Beamish spoke: "And what if, sir, the Germans don't intend to give us the slip? They're steaming right at us."

"How long have we been taking on coal? How much do we have?"

"Weeks replied: "Sir, we started at 0500. We're two-thirds full."

Famous for his unflappable nature, Sturdee thought only a second before issuing his first set of orders. "Very well, we'll risk it. *Kent* to weigh and proceed out to guard the harbor entrance. Cast aside all colliers. All other ships to raise steam for full speed and report when ready to sail."

· · ·

After saying this Sturdee went down for breakfast. He may not have been as calm on the inside as the image of coolness that he projected. Startled and confused, the British admiral was still not thinking clearly. Graf Spee had sent two ships to seize Port Stanley, *Gneisenau* and *Nürnberg*, which at full speed could get within range of the roadstead in less than an hour. Sturdee did not have the luxury to wait for two hours while his boiler crews worked the engines up to full heat and pressure. This work could also be done while the cruiser squadron put to sea. He may have had less speed, but as Captain Müller knew instinctively at the Cocos, less speed trumped sitting dead-duck-like at anchor.

Sturdee finished his breakfast as *Gneisenau* and her light cruiser escort drew within eight miles of Hooker's Point. When he returned on deck it was 0845. HMS *Kent*, the only ship in harbor with steam up, but little coal, began to move out of Port William behind the long, seven-mile tongue of land that extends east to the lighthouse. With the same inadequate armament as the deceased *Monmouth*, did she have a better chance against *Gneisenau*?"

Somewhat more to his credit, Sturdee issued new orders as the minutes ticked away to 0900. He ordered *Kent*, which had neared the lighthouse but had no fighting chance, to turn about. *Canopus*, whose captain, feeling abandoned, had asked if he could open fire, got orders to do this when the two raiders pulled within range of his 12-inch guns. Sturdee still hesitated to get the rest of his ships underway, gambling irresponsibly that he could wait another hour until all ships had steam up, but at least he signaled them: "Be ready to open fire at any moment." The Battle of the Falklands looked like it was going to be, as Wellington said of Waterloo, "a close-run thing."

• • •

Meanwhile, high atop the foremast of *Gneisenau*, Lieutenant Commander Johann Busche, chief gunnery officer, had been observing the harbor as best he could through the thick clouds of coal dust. The heavy cruiser sailed due north toward the light house, but the heading brought her gradually closer to Hooker's Point off the port bow. Initially, still 18,000 yards from the wireless station, he thought the British burned their coal stocks, as the French had done at Papeete. By 0845, now 14,000 yards from Hooker's Point, he issued final instructions to the turret crews, whose barrels swung four points to port and rose to maximum elevation, aiming at the wireless mast. Busche also telephoned the bridge that he identified *Glasgow* and *Bristol* in the inner harbor as well as *Monmouth*'s sister ship, *Kent*, as she made for the entrance to Port William.

But he had more to report. "Captain, I see warship masts farther back in the roadstead. Looks like *at least* two county class armored cruisers. They're not burning their coal stocks—we've caught a whole squadron coaling!"

Hearing this, Maerker spoke calmly into his phone: "Open fire on the wireless mast when we pass at 10,000 yards, Busche." He hung up that phone and picked up a phone to the engine room: "All ahead full," then hung up again. Turning to Pochhammer, and smiling, the captain boasted confidently: "We'll give *Kent* a taste of what her sister got at Coronel." Finally, he phoned the wireless room: "Wire the flagship: 'Have identified two light cruisers and several older armored cruisers coaling at Port Stanley. I am going to attack the enemy."

Busche called again: "Sir, it's difficult to see clearly through the dust, but the two ships farthest back in the roadstead appear to have three-legged tripod masts. This can only mean two battle cruisers!"

Maerker shook his head in disbelief: "Busche, that's impossible! That the enemy has ships here is no surprise to me, but the British have no battle cruisers in the South Atlantic!"

"That's what it looks like from up here, captain."

Maerker still did not believe him: "It must be that queen-class battleship we've known about, and another like her." He hung up, thought this over briefly, and then, agreeing with his own logic, not that of his man atop, turned to Pochhammer: "Number One, go to the radio room and wire *Scharnhorst*: 'Two queen-class battleships coaling with rest of English squadron'—and then get into the central control station."

And that moment, before the first officer could move, two big shells exploded in the water about two hundred yards to port. Maerker grabbed his phone and yelled into it: "Busche, what the hell was that!?"

"Heavy ordnance from behind the wireless station."

Canopus had fired her forward turret at 0920. The gun crews fore had not loaded blank projectiles yet, so these were live shells. The aft turret had blanks already in the barrels—this crew, eager to outdo the forward crew in the morning shoot, had loaded the practice shells secretly in the middle of the night. When ordered to fire, the aft turret commander phoned Captain Grant the bad news that his rifles had only blank rounds. Grant barked back: "Fire them anyway—and fire them now!"

Busche phoned again: "Incoming from shore battery." Maerker, who had already moved to the left side of the bridge to inspect Hooker's Point through his glasses, lowered them in time to see the shells hit the water fifty yards away. One of them ricocheted off the water and slammed into the second funnel with a loud metallic thud. "We're lucky—it was a dud," said the skipper with some relief. He ordered the helmsman: "Steer away four points to starboard."

· · ·

On the English side, meanwhile, tension reigned as one ship after another got word of the approaching Germans. As this news buzzed through HMS *Inflexible* between 0800 and 0830, Sturdee's second battle cruiser continued coolly to take on coal while work in the boiler rooms accelerated. Finishing breakfast at half past the hour, the chief gunnery officer, First Lieutenant Rudolf Verner, went to his station in the forecastle. When *Canopus* fired at 0920 he moved to the fore-top, received the order "get ready to open fire," and contemplated how to help his gunners hit targets he could see but they could not because of the peninsula obstructing their view—Churchill had yanked both ships away from Devonport before the upgrade of their foremast director-firing system had been completed.

Just then he caught sight of *Gneisenau* and *Nürnberg* across the spit of land leading to the light house—they were a mere 18,000 yards away, only minutes from being in range, and their gunners would have no comparable trouble with indirect fire. Farther south three patches of smoke marked Graf Spee's position.

"My first thoughts on hearing of the enemy's approach," recalled Verner, "were of bewilderment at our enormous good fortune in having arrived at Port Stanley in time, and at the enemy having the courtesy to come to us and to save us the long hunt we were prepared for. Second thoughts, however, were not so cheerful. Here we were in harbor, colliers alongside, steam available at about an hour's notice, most of us short of coal, and an apparently very enterprising enemy closing on us fast."

"Indirect fire at moving objects is not an artillerist's ideal, and in any case a squadron getting underway and going out of harbor under fire is not an ardently wished-for situation. I felt a distinct identification with the young man of these parts that a bard had written about: 'There was a young man of Cape Horn who wished he'd never been born.' Judging by the 'cheeriness' of everyone else, this young man must have been on other people's minds as well as my own."

•   •   •

On the bridge of *Scharnhorst*, Admiral Spee had received both wireless reports from *Gneisenau*. He paced back and forth, deep in thought. Finally, he made known his decision to First Officer Heinrich Bender: "Wire *Gneisenau*: 'Do not engage the enemy; rejoin the squadron at your best speed.'"

As Bender's jaw dropped incredulously, Captain Schultz spoke up: "Admiral, may I advise?"

Graf Spee cast Schultz a thunderbolt glance for a long moment, but then relented: "Go ahead, Schultz."

"Admiral—Sir!—if we attack without delay we've got them 'Copenhagened.' They're at anchor, coaling with no steam up. And even if they try to escape we can destroy them one by one as they exit the harbor—we'll cross their T. It will be a greater victory than Coronel!"

Graf Spee barely tolerated this advice. "Schultz, calm down." The admiral no doubt realized at this moment that a day earlier Maerker had been right and he wrong. But at least this time he did not let fatalism and indifference to fate elbow rationalism out of the way: "I wanted Port Stanley, not a sea battle so far away from Germany. We'll shoot up too many shells, and their battleships, while old, can still do damage. We'll outrun them and turn back after nightfall for the Argentine coast and our colliers."

He turned away to give it all some more thought for a full, tense minute. Finally he turned and pointed menacingly at Bender: "Send the wire—and send it now!"

• • •

It was about 0930 hours—a critical time for the fate of each squadron. Over the last forty-eight hours both the Germans and British made decisions in the absence of good intelligence—in the so-called fog of war. Sturdee had no idea that enemy warships had sailed almost to "his doorstep," but should have guessed as much from earlier reports, and still could have bought himself those crucial two hours of steaming-up time if he had had patrols out—both his light cruisers had finished coaling the day before. As for Graf Spee, with little to go on but old reports he ignored four of his five ship captains, who pointed out the risks of trying to capture Port Stanley.

Maerker, on the other hand, having correctly warned about the likelihood of combat in the Falklands, now cast fairly good intelligence aside: he ignored the advice of a trusted officer, one of the true heroes of Coronel, who saw big, fast, powerful battle cruisers—Busche was fairly certain what he had seen. Maerker had put Graf Spee in the position, while making his own decision—a *huge* disservice—of assuming that only slow, obsolete ships sat at anchor in the roadstead of Port William. Surely he could outrun them.

If Maerker had trusted in Busche, however, and relayed this intelligence to *Scharnhorst*, what would Spee have done? With no chance to outrun the bigger and faster battle cruisers, and facing the now inevitable expenditure of shells he had so wanted to avoid, Graf Spee, with a probability bordering on certainty, would have maximized his chances in disadvantageous circumstances and attacked with his entire squadron. He had risked it in Samoa, so why not now?

His chances looked good, in fact, against ships exposed to the terribly accurate fire of the German 8.2-inch gun crews and extremely vulnerable to the dangerous torpedoes of the light cruisers. Sturdee was truly "Copenhagened." With no chance to utilize his superior speed, and with little room to maneuver in the crowded roadstead, the likely fate of the British flotilla would have justified the chill that went up Churchill's spine about two hours later.

XXIV
OFF THE FALKLANDS

Gneisenau and Nürnberg took off without even firing a parting salvo at Hooker's Point. They steered east-southeast and rejoined their mates at 1040 hours. All five ships continued on this heading, assuming calmly that a storm in the normally stormy environs of the Falklands, or eventually nightfall, would guarantee their easy escape. But their pursuers were not obsolete queen class battleships easily left behind—the greyhounds would catch the hares.

When they did, would British speed and greater weight of shells or Spee's tactical brilliance and superior German gunnery decide the day? Although both sides had German-made stereoscopic range finders, ideal for long-range fighting, the Royal Navy, unlike the German Imperial Navy, had only recently installed them and had not practiced firing at 16,000 to 18,000 yards. Both British battle cruisers had calibrated their 12-inch guns with the plotting room below, and with the turrets, but as noted earlier, the installation of their fire control system had not been completed when they hurriedly left England in November. Worse still, while underway to the South Atlantic the guns had been calibrated for battle at only 12,000 yards, and the crews, even at this shorter distance, had had precious little target practice—they had had more at 6,000.

The British, therefore, would try to close the range to *under 12,000 yards*, but this would play into Graf Spee's hands. At this range his 8.2-inch mounts could do considerable damage to a fast but thinly armored battle cruiser. Moreover, at 12,000 yards his secondary armament of 5.9 inch guns came into range and could out duel Sturdee's 4-inch secondary guns before they could fire for effect. Finally, Graf Spee went into battle with fairly well-stocked magazines. Some sources report that each armored cruiser had 550 (of 800) 8.2-inch shells, while other sources put the figure at closer to 440, but both ships had full magazines of 5.9-inch shell, 600 apiece. Thus, despite British advantages on paper in some respects, the upcoming sea battle would likely be closely contested.

• • •

At 1030 hours, shortly before the German squadron got back together, all of Sturdee's ships except *Bristol*, which had some engine issues, left Port William. *Glasgow* had steamed away twenty minutes earlier to make sure the Germans did not slip from view.

Over the last hour many Kelpers had walked up to Sapper Hill to get a better look. Some drooled over the prospect of watching the Royal Navy put to death the alien menace that for a solid month had threatened their homes and families. This was to be a public execution. But even among those bent on revenge, and certainly among those with the closest ties to the

British sailors, anger mixed with concern for the safety of friends—nobody took the redoubtable East Asiatic lightly after Coronel. Mathilda and Anne Mari Haga, both in their nurse's uniforms, had thronged there with the rest—some two hundred people, including Allardyce. Like many atop the hill, they were worried.

One older woman shook her fist at the escaping German ships: "That'll teach yer for comin' muckin' 'round here!" Catching sight of HMS *Glasgow* racing ahead of the squadron, another woman screamed: "Look'y there, Guv, that one's takin' on the fat beer-drinkin' lauts all by 'isself!"

Hearing this, Anne Mari turned in horror to her mother: "My God, Mama, Lloyd's on *Glasgow*! They should wait for the bigger ships! They'll get killed!"

Mathilda, coming unraveled herself, but thinking of only one thing to say, hugged her daughter. "Captain Luce, Lloyd, and the officers of *Glasgow* know what they're doing, my dear ... they know what they're doing ... surely they do."

Many of the others now cheered the courageous charge of the light cruiser. Mother and daughter, however, hugged tighter and cried. Mathilda had convinced neither herself nor Anne Mari.

· · ·

With *Glasgow* scouting ahead to port and eager for revenge, Sturdee's squadron cleared the lighthouse and turned to the southeast to bag their quarry. The admiral raised the flag from his mast: "Give-General-Chase." The older cruisers tried to keep up, but could not. Sturdee reduced speed for them, but this allowed the East Asiatic to pull farther away. Sturdee knew what he had to do: the older armored cruisers seemed largely irrelevant, so he ordered: "Full ahead." *Invincible* and *Inflexible*, creating two huge clouds of smoke, pulled away from the old, antiquated ships Fisher and Cradock had condemned as "too weak to fight, too slow to run away."

• • •

HMS *Invincible*: The lead greyhound
(Imperial War Museum)

With the sun rising higher above us, we saw two vessels detach themselves from the number of our pursuers.[18] They seemed much bigger and faster than the others, as their smoke was thicker, wider, and more massive. All glasses focused inquisitively and then anxiously on their hulls and masts, which were almost completely enveloped by smoke. At first it seemed only a slight possibility, but then as the minutes passed a good probability that we were being chased by battle cruisers.

"Are they Japanese?" said Captain Maerker, still refusing to believe that the English had moved theirs so far south. I did not think the Japanese would risk their precious ships so far away from their real interests in the Far East. But then, before any time for debate, Busche phoned down to confirm that these were indeed English battle cruisers.

We had no more claim to be treated with velvet gloves than our countrymen fighting in Europe, but it was a very big and bitter pill to swallow. Were we to be condemned under the old law of naval warfare which ordains that the less powerful and the less swift should be vanquished in free waters and fine weather? We choked a little at the neck, the throat contracted and stiffened—we felt real fear.

But we soon shook it off and prepared to set a good example for the men. The captains warned their crews that the fighting would be hot. We awaited the following hours calmly, full of a rock-solid desire to fight like true Germans, and if it came to it, to die like true Germans.

---

18   From Pochhammer, *Before Jutland*. See my methodological Afterword.

. . .

Invincible took the lead with *Inflexible* astern to port. By 1230 hours, steering to the southeast at 26 knots, they had closed the distance from fifteen to ten miles—17,250 yards. They sailed upwind of the trailing German ship, *Leipzig*, with *Dresden*, *Scharnhorst*, *Nürnberg*, and *Gneisenau* ahead of her in line, all racing at 22 knots. At 1247 Sturdee ran up the flags for "Engage-the-Enemy," and a few minutes later both battle cruisers opened fire with their forward 12-inch "A" turrets at 16,500 yards. The first salvos fell badly short, but gradually, as the time drew on to 1315 and the range narrowed a little, salvos began to straddle *Leipzig*.

At 1320 another one almost hit her bow. Seeing this, Graf Spee thought for a few seconds, not least about his son Otto on *Nürnberg*, which strained and struggled due to boiler problems to keep pace. Suddenly the admiral grabbed a signalman by the arm and drew him closer: "Send to all three light cruisers: 'Light cruisers leave the line and try to escape—act independently. Heavy cruisers will accept action.' "

A father was going to save at least one of his sons—and hopefully most of his command. To the helmsman he ordered: "Hard to port—steer east-northeast." And to the signalman: "To *Gneisenau*: 'Steer east-northeast. Concentrate fire with *Scharnhorst* on the enemy flagship.' "

Over the next forty-five minutes the two lines converged from 16,000 to 12,000 yards, both sides firing as quickly as they could once the range narrowed. The

German cruisers, however, discharged their big guns at twice the rate of the British.

•   •   •

Glasgow had doubled back and turned south to chase Spee's light cruisers. As she passed around and astern of Sturdee's battle cruisers, Higgs and Thompson observed the battle.

"At this rate," said Higgs to Thompson, "it looks as if Sturdee and not Von Spee is going to be sunk."

"It's certainly damned bad shooting," replied Number One with remarkably little emotion as he finished tapping a cigarette and lit up.

•   •   •

We were confident that Sturdee with his powerful 12-inch guns would make as short work of Von Spee as the latter had made of Cradock.[19] As we turned to the south under the stern of *Inflexible*, however, we saw the rippling flashes and rapid disciplined fire of the enemy's guns at what must have been his extreme range. Nonetheless, the splashes were too close to *Invincible*, upon whom the two German cruisers appeared to be concentrating, for my liking.

Sturdee's hastily-lit boilers, full of oil-sprayed coal, were pouring out thick volumes of smoke from the funnels, and the slight southeasterly wind was blowing this and the cordite fumes from the guns along the line of sighting of both ships, obstructing observance of the

---

19   From Hirst, *Coronel and After*. See my methodological Afterword.

fall of shots and aiming of guns. *Inflexible*, leeward of *Invincible*, had frequently to suspend fire until finally deciding to haul out on her leader's starboard quarter to try to get clear of the smoke.

A little later we crossed under the sterns of the German ships, far off to port, and were able to see what little punishment they were getting. We were dismayed at the battle cruisers' gunnery, the slow and ragged fire, the loose pattern with an occasional shot falling close, but most of the others flying far over or falling far short. The impression I got was that each turret was in "local" control, the primary control system having failed. My heart sank into my boots—were the upstart Germans once again going to humiliate the Royal Navy?!

• • •

The time was now 1340, ten minutes into the battle. Atop *Invincible*'s foremast Lieutenant Commander Edward Dannreuter, the chief gunnery officer, cursed to his assistant spotter the adverse circumstances he faced: "How the hell are we supposed to hit 'em if we can't see 'em!"

Just then the bridge rang through. Dannreuter responded to the anxious question from below: "I can't see well enough to say whether or not we've hit them even once! The wind is blowing our smoke down range! Their short shots are sending up columns of water right in the line of sighting! Engine vibrations and the salvos of A-Turret right below us make my new range-finder useless—I can't focus on anything! The lads down in the plotting room must be bloody bored—I can't pass anything along to them!"

He paused to hear the next question, and responded: "All right, shifting fire control to the turrets. I'll help out from here as best I can."

•   •   •

On the bridge of *Scharnhorst*, Graf Spee nervously awaited news of a first hit. The gunnery spotter phoned down to Schultz, who listened, hung up, and then passed along the information to the admiral: "All shots falling short."

"Steer north-northeast, Schultz. We have to close the range."

Schultz ordered the helmsman: "Four points to port."

At 1345, as admiral and captain and spotter peered anxiously through their glasses, the latter yelled into his phone: "Direct hit amidships. The smoke makes it nearly impossible to say for sure, but I think we did damage to an armored tower above the enemy conning tower."

Those on the bridge strained to see what would happen next. "He's turning away. Is he disengaging?" remarked Graf Spee, spoiling himself for just a moment with an optimistic speculation. "Turn about, Schultz, and head due south."

Schultz so instructed the helmsman. Next he phoned the first officer for a damage report. Maerker followed the same procedure on *Gneisenau* and signaled the flagship. A few minutes later Schultz relayed good news to the top man: "Sir, no significant dam-age to either of us. Fighting strength—all guns, all boiler rooms—at full capacity."

. . .

We did not follow the English.[20] On the contrary, at 1405 hours Graf Spee wheeled to the south, the direction one might expect bad weather to come. In fact, during this turn we could see that the sky ahead of us had darkened. Every minute we gained before we could disappear into the storm, or into the night, might decide our fate. The engines were still in tact and doing their best.

The antagonists moved away from each other at great speed. Soon we were out of the range of their big ordnance. We rapidly repaired the slight damage and debris from the first action, anything that might get in the way of the next, for the enemy was in no humor to leave us much time—he too had wheeled around and was pursuing us again. Slowly but surely the two battle cruisers gained on us.

Their lead ship opened fire at 18,500 yards. We could not reply at this distance. Although the enemy shells fell right in front of us, and across the bow of Scharnhorst, our admiral calmly waited until the range-finders registered 16,250 yards, and then we both swung hard to port. The range decreased rapidly. At 1445 we made ranging shots at 14,000 yards. Within minutes the range narrowed to around 11,000 yards. Our fire quickened.

---

20   From Pochhammer, Before Jutland. See my methodological Afterword.

•   •   •

In his spotting station high up in the fore mast, Dannreuter observed the German's maneuver through the smoke that still clouded his view. "Good tactics," he said to the assistant spotter, "he's closing the range and trying to cross our T."

Over the next few minutes, as enemy salvos got closer, and British too, he watched as *Invincible* copied the enemy's turn by steering hard to port. At 1455, he phoned to the bridge: "Our lads finally have the mark. Several direct hits on both enemy cruisers!"

A second after Dannreuter hung up, *Scharnhorst*'s first salvo found the mark too. A few shells plummeted short, but one blew away the fore mast strut, making the observation truck wobble and sway with every movement of the ship. Both men up top looked at one another anxiously. Three shells coming in at steep angles of descent like the others exploded high up in the superstructure and upper deck area, causing considerable damage. Fear would be no stranger to either side in this battle—now English throats tightened.

Five seconds later *Gneisenau* found the range. Her shells also tore into superstructure and holed funnels, but one pierced the upper deck and exploded in the empty wardroom, destroying it and every object in it. And then, a few seconds later, *Scharnhorst*'s next broadside sent four shells just over, but two scored direct hits: one pierced the armor belt of the bow at the water line; the other holed *Invincible* ten feet under the water line amidships four decks below the starboard "P" turret. Both made loud metallic clanks, like hammer hitting anvil. The ship shuddered.

On the bridge anxiety seized Sturdee. Seeing his admiral coming unnerved, Flag Captain Beamish picked up a phone: "Engineer Commander, assess damage at the water line and report back." As he hung up, another shell hit right in front of the armored conning tower, knocking Dannreuter down but again sparing the shaky fore mast. Beamish rang up his spotter: "Dannreuter, do what you can to increase our rate of fire. What the devil can we do to sink these bastards! "

Just then another incoming salvo hit, blowing away a lifeboat to the right of the tower, a second shell hitting the top of "A" turret but not bursting, others hitting higher up. Sturdee had seen enough: "They've hit us 15 or 20 times—and that's 15-to-20 too many! 360 degree turn to port," he ordered the helmsman. "We'll cross under their sterns."

A moment later the phone rang on the bridge. Captain Beamish picked it up and listened for a moment. "Thank you Weeks," he said and hung up. "Admiral, we're holed fore and amidships. Bow compartments flooded, "P" bunker flooded, slight list to starboard. But sir—neither of these shells burst."

"We almost blew a magazine?"

"Bloody close to it, admiral. The shell made a large hole in the hull and then broke up against the interior armor of the magazine handling room."

All of these near misses got to the normally unflappable Sturdee. "They almost blew "A" turret too. Good thing there's something wrong with their fuses today.

Otherwise there'd be something bloody wrong with our ship," he exclaimed.

"They took it hard on the chin that round, admiral. They can't last much longer."

This made Sturdee feel a little better. "Let's hope so, Beamish, let's hope so."

Indeed, from their vantage point miles away both Dannreuter and Beamish believed they saw their opponent in this heavy weight bout weakening from the battle cruisers' pounding body punches. Neither had seen as many columns of water shooting up from short salvos as before, but rather ominous-looking flashes and puffs of smoke, clear indications of shells detonating against metal.

However, the East Asiatic, utilizing its rapid, accurate fire, had come within three fuse flukes of blasting *Invincible* sky high, avoiding more of Sturdee's damaging body shots, winning the action quickly, and preserving precious shells. Fisher's greyhounds had been built for speed, sacrificing vital inches of armor belt to catch fast ships like *Scharnhorst* and *Gneisenau*. But on this day speed had brought Sturdee's flagship dangerously close to the disastrous end she met at the Battle of Jutland eighteen months later.

If this had occurred would *Inflexible* have fought on, hoping to sink the enemy cruisers before their concentrated fire sank her too? And if she too had blown up, what would Churchill have done? If two battle cruisers could not do the job would he have dispatched dreadnoughts into the South Atlantic? And then what would have taken place in the North Sea? What Beatty and Jellicoe feared, and Tirpitz yearned for? Lest we forget, earlier that morning Graf Spee had opted not to maul whatever lay at anchor in Port Stanley—twice in one day he had come so very close to victories pregnant with major repercussions for the outcome of the Great War at sea.

•   •   •

It was by now 1515 hours. Observing Sturdee's turn from the bridge of *Scharnhorst*, Spee immediately issued new orders to his helmsman: "Hard to port. Steady her on southwest." He turned to Schultz: "I await the damage reports."

For a second time the German cruisers pulled away from their hunters. *Gneisenau* steamed off the starboard bow of her flagship. With the second action over, Pochhammer exited his "steel dungeon" to make a quick inspection round. Sailors raced around the ship trying to ready a fighter's bloody body for the next round. His first glances fore and aft revealed the terrible beating the ship had taken: funnels holed and askew, superstructure torn up, fires all over, which the crew was trying to extinguish, and evidence of the horrific human carnage—limbs and heads torn off and strewn about, pools of blood, and brain splatters on bulkheads. A 12-inch shell had obliterated the radio room. Another had flooded an engine room with the stokers in it. A third had hit one of the sick bays filled with wounded sailors, their misery now over.

He hurried toward the bridge, but suddenly looking off to port the first officer stopped in his tracks. The sight of *Scharnhorst*, which looked even worse than her sister, shocked and upset him: multiple fires, huge holes in her hull, two funnels blown away with white steam hissing out, a list to port, and already down at the bows ten degrees. A day that had begun so promisingly had come to this?

Pochhammer found Maerker on the port captain's bridge surveying the stricken sibling ship. He motioned the signalman to come over: "To the flagship: 'Why is the admiral's flag at half mast? Is he dead?' "

The signalman waited for the reply, finally saying: "The admiral replies: 'I am all right so far. What have you hit?' "

Maerker replied: "To the flagship: 'The smoke is so bad it is impossible to tell.' "

Neither German cruiser could make more than 18 knots at this point in the battle, while the British ships, having also turned about, quickly sped up to 26 knots. By 1540 hours Sturdee had once again gotten into range northeast of the injured hares and opened fire. The same southeasterly wind now cleared smoke to port, allowing first *Inflexible* a clear view of targets, and then, after *Invincible* overtook her, the flagship. By steering southwest toward his light cruisers Graf Spee had made a fatal tactical mistake.

As enemy salvos got closer and closer, *Scharnhorst* reversed course and charged "death-ride-style" toward the enemy. On *Gneisenau*, Maerker wondered out loud: "Is he trying to close for torpedoes?"

Seconds later a signalman interrupted Maerker with something coming from the bridge of the flagship: "Sir, the flag sends: 'You were right after all, my friend. Try to escape.' " Maerker knew the meaning of this message—Graf Spee had apologized for his mistake of not avoiding the Falklands altogether, coaling at Puerto Santa Elena, totally eluding the greyhounds, escaping safely into the North Atlantic, and perhaps making it home. The admiral's friend, feeling sheepish about his own deadly errors, did not reply. Rather, he came to attention and saluted *Scharnhorst* as she limped courageously away to the northeast.

The British pummeled the German ship mercilessly. They had no choice: her top flags still flew, and she kept firing. At 1617 hours *Scharnhorst*'s fore turret, water already over the bow just a few feet from the barrels, fired one last time. And then the proud ship fell over on her port side, propellers rising out of the sea, and slid beneath the waves. In one afternoon Graf Spee and the entire ship's company of 800 officers and men perished.

The end for *Gneisenau* beckoned. The battle cruisers, joined at last by armored cruiser *Carnavon*, closed in for the kill, silencing one gun after another with direct hits, compounding the already devastating damage to the ship and adding to the horrific loss of life. At 1715 the battered ship fired one last shot that hit and exploded but did not penetrate *Invincible*'s armor belt. Because *Gneisenau* listed badly to starboard—in fact she was slowly capsizing—Maerker ordered abandon ship.

• • •

The captain ordered us to go on deck and secure life buoys and other flotation devices.[21] The men left

---

21   From Pochhammer, *Before Jutland*. See my methodological Afterword.

their stations in perfect order and carried the wounded above. I wanted to be the last to leave the central station, but the second torpedo officer remained there behind me, explaining that he had as yet received no orders to evacuate the torpedo rooms, which could mean, against all odds, that Maerker had not decided to give up the fight and would close for a torpedo run. Such loyalty of officers and men goes without saying in the navy, even in a foundering ship, but this man's steadfastness fills me with awe to this day.

I left the officer behind me, telling him to follow as quickly as possible, and climbed through the dark and narrow shaft to the blockhouse under the bridge. As I did, my thoughts turned for a moment to the ex-petty officer from Kiel who had joined our torpedo crews in Valparaiso. Of 800 men, I thought of him, but this was not so strange. Bauer was quite popular with the men after his iceberg remark, but there was more. When I warned all of the new recruits that the next fight could be hotter than Coronel *he* had spoken up for all of them: "It's all the same to us, captain, we want to go with you." Would he and the rest of the torpedo crews make it out?

•   •   •

Pochhammer knew that he would soon become his ship's senior officer. Around 1730 hours he did his best to supervise as 250 unwounded men helped 150 of their wounded shipmates down the portside hull into an icy, 38-degree ocean. Maerker stayed on board and went down with his ship at exactly 1800. Heinrich von Spee and at least 400 others, already dead or dying or trapped below decks, went down with him.

Pochhammer and other officers helped the sailors form into small groups of six or seven until the British ships could draw near and lower boats, which could not happen quickly. Salty arctic water needles pricked and plunged into every one of the survivors, whose painful battle was not over. Some had life jackets, others a hammock with an air pocket that helped, still others only an oar or piece of debris. Hyperthermia sets in very quickly at such frigid temperatures, however, and one after another the men seized up. With strength dwindling rapidly, they were cursed further by attacking albatrosses that dove ravenously at their watery prey. Those with oars swung madly at the black monsters—some men were saved in this way, others were pecked to death.

Only 170 men, Pochhammer among them, made it into British boats. The rescue craft that saved the freezing first officer had steered between two groups of Germans and begun to pull men in from both sides. Pochhammer insisted that the three survivors from his circle get in first. After a few additional minutes in the water he no longer had the strength to climb in.

Just then, however, one of the German sailors already in the boat yelled out to the others: "Come lads, let's give our first officer a hand!" Pochhammer looked up: it was Johannes Bauer, looking surprisingly little the worse for wear.

The rescue boats rowed slowly to *Invincible*. Crew members went down the hull to help the Germans up. Above them along the railings hundreds of shocked

British victors stared at the bodies of well over a hundred dead men still floating—another hundred or so, no longer with the strength to tread water, had sunk— and at the big birds still feeding. Although out of the ice cold water and finally away from the albatrosses, 70 German sailors who had lost too much body heat died during the night. Of 800 hands on *Gneisenau* only 100 lived.

Pochhammer and Bauer were among the lucky few. One returned to Germany to publish his story, grow old with his family, and bounce grandchildren on his lap. The other returned to Valparaiso less naïve about war and more committed to life. He had a bank to run, a marriage to arrange, and a family to start.

· · ·

Since leaving the two battle cruisers shortly after 1300 hours, Captain Luce had circled back around the bigger ships and steamed full speed to the southwest in pursuit of the German light cruisers. *Glasgow* opened fire at the closest, SMS *Leipzig*, around 1500, scoring a lucky hit from very long range. Because the British cruiser was four or five knots faster, her stern chase steadily shortened the distance. Finally, around 1700 hours, with the range at 12,000 yards, *Leipzig* turned hard to starboard and fired her first broadside, scoring hits but causing no significant damage. Because she had turned, however, freeing up all starboard guns, the range continued to narrow and armored cruiser *Cornwall*, although old and lumbering, caught up to the action.

As late afternoon yielded to evening rainfall and the gradual onset of darkness, the battle intensified. From 10,000 yards the greater weight of British 6-inch shell tore into *Leipzig*, one hit after another holing her, knocking over a funnel, setting fires, and mangling the superstructure. At 1945 she ceased fire and began to assemble those still alive, about two hundred officers and men, in boats and on deck for rescue by the victorious enemy. *Glasgow* drew closer, ready to save survivors.

•   •   •

Meanwhile, armored cruiser *Kent* had conducted a stern chase of her own. Under normal circumstances she would never have been able to close the distance to SMS *Nürnberg*, but the German cruiser had fire in only ten boilers, two having burst. The obsolete British ship opened fire at 1700 hours from 12,000 yards. Over the next two hours, with both vessels in parallel converging battle line, the action grew hotter and hotter, the range closing to a mere 6,000 yards.

Both sides took a beating, *Nürnberg* suffering more damaging hits, but at 1900, after being hit over thirty times, *Kent* came close to sharing the fate of *Good Hope*. A German shell exploded in a casemate gun mount, igniting a stack of cordite charges. The flame flashed down the shell hoist into the handling room below. One of the handlers threw a charge away from the fire, however, and then extinguished the flames with a fire hose before they could blow up the room, and with it, the magazine.

Nürnberg continued the by-now one-sided fight for another half hour. Demolished and burning from a dozen fires, she sank at 1930. As she went under a group of sailors, defiant to the end, waved a battle ensign they had attached to a staff. *Kent* lowered boats for survivors, but there were only twelve, and five of these died of their wounds. Otto von Spee and nearly 390 others—almost the entire crew—perished.

•   •   •

Leipzig appeared to have been spared the same devastating fate—although about half of the crew was already dead or trapped below decks. Out of ammunition, she ceased fire and prepared to surrender 200 men. Scores of wounded sailors were placed in undamaged ship's boats, while the unhurt and walking wounded assembled on deck. The captain called out: "Anyone who likes to can haul down the colors." The men just looked at one another—none wanted to be the first to execute such a sadly humiliating order.

At that moment—around 1955 hours—a 4.1 inch cordite charge went off in the barrel of a gun, firing off the shell. Seconds later the same thing happened at another gun mount. Both charges had been ignited by nearby fires, but Captain Luce did not—and could not—have known this. He opened fire again, ripping *Leipzig* apart with six broadsides from point blank range. The wounded packed in lifeboats as well as unwounded crewmen standing so close together fell victim by the score with each shot—one shell alone killed sixty men. *Glasgow* finally ceased fire at 2030 and lowered boats, but *Leipzig*, her hull riddled with holes, funnels shot away, and upper deck a mass of twisted steel, soon went down by the bows. Only eleven German sailors got safely into the British ship.

For the rest of his days, Lloyd Higgs, like Luce, Thompson, and every officer and man aboard *Glasgow*, remembered the horrific destruction of SMS *Leipzig*. He never felt excessive sympathy or remorse, however, for war is war, after all, and in his war turnabout for Coronel added up to fair play. Higgs moved on. He, too, had a life to lead, a love to pursue, and a family to bring up.

• • •

The third German light cruiser, SMS *Dresden*, *Emden*-like fast, had sailed away to the southwest, not due south like *Leipzig* and *Nürnberg*, and thus managed to escape the Battle of the Falklands. *Glasgow*, *Cornwall*, and *Kent* searched nearby waters for her, but lost her in the darkness. *Dresden* steamed through the night back toward Cape Horn.

XXV
BLANKENBURG IN THE HARZ

"And so, dearest mother and father, I near the end of my story. Only Dresden got away from the carnage off the Falklands. This lone ship of our proud East Asiatic Squadron remained afloat. But Admiral Sturdee's avengers eventually caught up with her too, sending her down to join Scharnhorst, Gneisenau, Nürnberg, and Leipzig at the bottom of the ocean. Of ships' companies of 2,800 officers and men that had sailed from Valparaiso into history in November 1914, less than 500 lived to tell their tales. Most of these were from Dresden. The large part of her crew was able to abandon ship and thus avoid a cruel death at sea.

The same could not be said for SMS Karlsruhe, whose magazines exploded mysteriously in Barbados. She met her end five days before we did—if Graf Spee had made it to the Caribbean he would have searched for her in vain.

And what of those of us who had sailed west into the Indian Ocean? Most men of the Emden never saw home again either. Mücke and Lauterbach were among the lucky ones, but they made their own luck.

My first officer and fifty men of the landing party on Cocos Island commandeered a schooner and, after many harrowing adventures in the Indian Ocean, made landfall in Arabia. From there they went to Istanbul, and eventually back to the Fatherland. Lauterbach and the crew of our collier Exford were captured by the British and imprisoned in Singapore with the crew of our first collier, Markomannia, and those aboard Pontoporos. The big man led a daring prison break, however, and, like Mücke, returned home.

Most of my crew was not so fortunate. The Battle of the Cocos Islands killed or wounded 208 men. Only 117 of us were uninjured when the British brought us to our POW cells on Malta. We all suffered terribly from the guilt that the survivors of wars always feel.

Yes, our war was tragic, but after it ended for me, Graf Spee and his sons, and 2,500 sailors from the squadron who did not survive, things got worse, much worse—it is with good reason that they are calling it the 'Great War.' More than ten million soldiers will die before it is all over. Prisoners have not been taken. Unthinkable atrocities have been committed against civilians: hostages have been shot, innocents hung as assassins or spies, passenger liners sunk without warning, and whole peoples uprooted and driven mercilessly to their deaths—Jews, Poles, Greeks, and Armenians. And, as you know better than I, hundreds of thousands are dying of starvation and disease in Germany and Austria-Hungary during these years of Great Britain's merciless hunger blockade. There is no honor in this war. I am ashamed for humanity.

My parents, I fear for our times. The Great War has cut down the Russian monarchy, and it will fell both of our allied empires too. Later they may be reestablished and united, but it will surely happen under the evil banner of nationalistic fanatics who will trigger another great war that will scourge Europe and the world and inflict far higher human cost. And when that second great world war comes to an end the terrible weapons it will surely spawn—weapons much worse than our already terrible killing machines—will certainly grip the entire world in fear. And what if terrorists like those that Killed Archduke Ferdinand in 1914 acquire these weapons of truly mass destruction? There will never be peace in our time.

Alas, we played our role in starting all of this in 1914—we were so naïve and unexpecting. But all of us in every country opened this terrorizing Pandora's Box.

All of this happened under the teary eyes of God.

Will we, his children, ever learn?"

AFTERWORD ON HISTORICAL METHODOLOGY, SOURCES, GENRE, AND INTERPRETATION

I conceived this saga as a historical novel or, more accurately, a novelistic history. The idea of telling the story in this way came to me very early on in the process of researching and writing my most recent book, *A History of the Great War: World War One and the International Crisis of the Early Twentieth Century* (Oxford University Press, 2009). In this book and all of my previous works I substituted novelistic scenes or vignettes for the dry introductory paragraphs one finds in many history books—all to enhance readability. I based these scenes on primary source material and chose them to peak readers' curiosity about what follows in each chapter. Often I placed another vignette midway through a chapter. So it finally occurred to me to write a whole book this way, but I had been drifting toward writing history novelistically for many years.

Regardless of the presentational format, however, *Death at Sea* is nine parts history and only one part historical fiction. I have written it in keeping with the best of academic historical traditions. By academic history I mean the "German School" that arose in the mid-to-late 1800s and quickly spread to the universities of other nations, including the United States. The founder of this school, Leopold von Ranke, taught the importance—the outright imperative—of maintaining scientific objectivity while pursuing research in archival documents, accounts of participants, and other primary sources, the entire endeavor aiming to tell "what really happened."

One of Ranke's most brilliant students, Jakob Burckhardt, took his mentor's historical methodology, in my opinion, to a new height. In his masterpiece, *The Civilization of the Renaissance in Italy* (1860), Burckhardt immersed himself in the primary sources, but then, ignoring Ranke's overly cautious strictures against speculation, used his research-honed, documentation-informed instincts to interpret the historical evidence. His methodology was not as radical as it may seem to some, for Burckhardt, unlike Ranke, realized that gaps *always* exist between pieces of historical evidence and that all historians, whether they know it or not, make subjective assumptions about what is *not* there, somewhat like viewing a mosaic from ancient times with pieces missing and imagining, based on the parts one *can* see, what the whole mosaic must have looked like. In so doing, he painted a fuller and yet very accurate picture of the Renaissance.

•   •   •

The novelistic historical presentation of *Death at Sea* is firmly grounded, as Burckhardt would have done it, in a wealth of primary sources. The battles at sea are matters of the historical record based on the detailed post-combat action reports that are required in all navies.[22] Beyond these are the accounts of the survivors. The last cruise of SMS *Emden* emerges in private comments to friends and family made by her captain, Karl von Müller, as well as his unpublished report to the admiralty after his return to Germany in 1918.[23] There are also the detailed memoirs of Prince Hohenzollern, Helmuth von Mücke, and Julius Lauterbach. The remembrances of Hans Pochhammer, first officer of SMS *Gneisenau*, and one of his subordinates, Lieutenant Commander Joachim Lietzmann, are even more valuable. Graf Spee and his sons also wrote letters home to Countess Margarete that survived, as did much of the wartime correspondence of Gustav Maerker and Karl von

---

22   Most valuable for the Falklands are the reports of H. Edward Dannreuter, printed in Richard Hough, *The Pursuit of Admiral von Spee* (London, 1969), 171-175; and Rudolf Verner, *The Battle Cruisers at the Action of the Falkland Island* (London, 1920). For the Cocos Islands, see the reports of HMAS *Sydney*'s gunnery officer, Lieutenant Rahilly, cited in Dan van der Vat, *Gentlemen of War* (New York, 1983), 107-108, and another officer on board, Lieutenant Garcia, printed in R. K. Lochner, *The Last Gentlemen of War* (Annapolis, Maryland, 1988), 193-197. For Coronel, see Graf Spee's accounts in Hermann Kirchoff (ed.), *Maximilian Graf von Spee: Der Sieger von Coronel* (Berlin, 1915). For Coronel and the Falkalnds, also see reports excerpted in Geoffrey Bennett, *Coronel and Falklands* (London, 1965) and Hough, *Pursuit of Admiral von Spee*.
23   Discussed and cited at length in Van der Vat, *Gentlemen of War*, and Lochner, *Last Gentlemen of War* (cited above in Note 1), and especially Erich Raeder, *Die Kreuzerkrieg in den auslaendischen Gewaesser*, Volume 2: *Die Taetigkeit der Kleinkreuzer Emden, Königsberg und Karlsruhe* (Berlin, 1927).

Schönberg.[24] Moreover, great insights to the thinking of the German admiralty come from the memoirs of Naval Minister Alfred von Tirpitz, while on the British side a gold mine of documentation and recollections of discussions is found in First Lord of the Admiralty Winston Churchill's history of World War One.[25] Finally, the life of the sailors of HMS *Glasgow* on the Falklands and their experiences in battle come forth in great detail in the memoirs of two officers, Lloyd Hirst and Harold Hickling.[26]

From these documents and accounts (and others cited below) the history you have read springs. In the vast majority of cases the dialogue is based on what was actually said—Cradock's laments before leaving the Falklands in October 1914, Graf Spee's remarks in Valparaiso in November, or the comments of Allardyce, Luce, Thompson, and Sturdee to mention just a few examples. At other times—for instance, Spee's conference with his officers on Pagan Island in August—I know what was discussed, which sides were taken, and by whom, even some of what was actually

---

24   Franz Joseph von Hohenzollern, *Emden* (New York, 1920); Helmuth von Mücke, *Emden* (Berlin, 1915); Lowell Thomas (ed.), *Lauterbach of the China Sea* (London, 1930); Hans Pochhammer, *Graf Spee's letzte Fahrt: Erinnerungen an das Kreuzergeschwader* (Berlin, 1918), appearing in translation by H. J. Stenning as *Before Jutland: Graf Spee's Last Voyage* (London, 1931); Joachim Lietzmann, *Auf verlorenem Posten: Unter der Flagge des Grafen Spee* (Ludwigshafen am Bodensee, 1922); and Gerhard Wiechmann (ed.), *Vom Auslandsdienst in Mexico zur Seeschlacht von Coronel: Kapitaen zur See Karl von Schönberg Reisetagebuch 1913-1914* (Bochum, 2004) . For Graf Spee's letters and numerous recollections of his statements, see Kirchoff, *Maximilian Graf von Spee*.
25   Alfred von Tirpitz, *My Memoirs* (New York, 1919); Winston S. Churchill, *The World Crisis* (London, 1931).
26   Lloyd Hirst, *Coronel and After* (London, 1934); Harold Hickling, *Sailor at Sea* (London, 1965)

said, but for the rest I fill in the evidentiary gaps à la Burckhardt.

As for Karl von Müller, he swore he would never publish his story, and he did not, contenting himself with private comments, some of which were recorded, and his report to the admiralty. I use these to construct his narration, but for some of it I took the liberty of borrowing from Pochhammer's memoirs—the opening description of Tsingtao in 1914, for example, or his colorful descriptions of coaling at sea. There is nothing here, however, that Müller would not also have thought and observed. As for Pochhammer, much of his narration comes, sometimes verbatim, from his memoir. Methodologically, in my opinion, this is just like drawing on and citing a primary source—and I have used footnotes at these places of the text. However, I have taken the liberty of touching up and contemporizing the English. I have also added at times to his memoir, as in the references to Johannes Bauer.

• • •

One of my main goals in writing *Death at Sea* was to emphasize the depth of catastrophe. This is why I first introduced the German characters, allowing readers to sympathize with them; moving the British characters on stage next, again allowing readers to gain sympathy; and finally bringing both character sets together in bloody battles. By "feeling the pain" of both camps readers can focus on the terrible losses suffered by each and appreciate, without the patriotic blinders of that day, the very real tragedy of the First World War.

One—tragedy—is no stranger to the other—war—but this story is extreme "Senecan" tragedy. Seneca, the ancient Roman playwright, usually dispatched most of his cast before the end of the last act, and so it was with 1914's first tragic naval actions. British death rates at Coronel and German at the Falklands were horrific: between seventy- and seventy-five percent.

The Senecan saga of the German East Asiatic Squadron and its British pursuers also intersected in a very real way, however, with *the people* of two towns, Port Stanley and Valparaiso. Civilians there lived through the tragedy of the Great War's first year too, experiencing the same kind of drama, Angst, and romantic yearnings that are so well described in Pochhammer's memoirs.

So how to tell this latter day tale of two cities? How to do justice to the emotions felt by so very, very many? The appropriate genre, it seemed to me, was a historical fiction of sorts, but here too I used primary sources to capture the moods and emotions in these towns.

For example, in the case of Lloyd Higgs and his "up home" family in Port Stanley, the Hagas, Higgs' character is modeled closely on the actual communications officer of *Glasgow*, Lloyd Hirst, whose memoirs I have used, sometimes verbatim, for his narrations. But I have also drawn closely, sometimes verbatim, on the memoirs of Harold Hickling, a younger officer whose recollections reveal much more about social life in port. Higgs, in other words, is a composite of Hirst and Hickling. Methodologically, my use of these memoirs may seem somewhat unorthodox, but, like the narrative passages on the German side of the story, I look at this as very similar to a historian who draws on and cites primary source material—here too I used footnotes at the appropriate places.

The second case of historical fiction is that of Johannes Bauer and Simone von Eichhorn. We know from Pochhammer's memoirs that an ex-petty officer from the 1st Torpedo Division at Kiel who had expatriated to Valparaiso and earned a good salary in a bank there signed on SMS *Gneisenau* after Coronel. That is all we know, but the Bauer-Eichhorn scenes, like the passages on the Falklands that accurately reflect life in the islands, are firmly grounded in the history of the German émigré community in Valparaiso, Hirst's recollections of his cold reception there on October 15th, and factual details from Pochhammer, Lietzmann, and Schönberg of the East Asiatic's visit on November 3rd-4th.

• • •

Embedded in this novelistic history and its two cases of historical fiction is my own interpretation of events. There are many fine secondary works that tell the story of the German and British squadrons that hunted one another across the Indian Ocean, the Pacific, and South Atlantic, but none of them does justice to the wider context of the war in its first year. [27]

---

27   In addition to the secondary works cited in Notes 1 and 2, see Fritz Otto Busch, *Admiral Spee's Sieg und Untergang* (Berlin, 1935); Barrie Pitt, *Coronel and Falkland* (London, 1960); Edwin P. Hoyt, *The Cruise of the Emden* (New York, 1966); Robin Bromby, *German Raiders of the South Sea* (Sydney, 1985); Harald Eschenburg, *Prinz Heinrich von Preussen: Der Grossadmiral im Schatten des Kaisers* (Heide, 1989); Keith Yates, *Graf Spee's Raiders: Challenge to the Royal Navy, 1914-1915* (Annapolis, Maryland, 1995); and Robert K. Massie, *Castles of Steel* (New York, 2003), 179-286.

For one thing, other historians have overlooked what was at stake in 1914 as Graf Spee made his decision on Pagan Island. If he had agreed with Müller and sailed west with the whole squadron and paralyzed the Indian Ocean, what choice would Churchill have had but to send a powerful squadron of battle cruisers and dreadnoughts to protect the heart of the empire, thereby greatly weakening the Grand Fleet in home waters and improving the odds of the German home fleet winning the war at sea? If Müller was right and Graf Spee wrong, in other words, we have a measure of sorts for the magnitude of the opportunity missed. As it was, *Emden* executed her mission remarkably well and certainly might have continued to plague British shipping were it not for her fuse debacle at the Cocos Islands—a fluky yet critical factor that no other historian has discussed.

We also need to ask what was riding on the East Asiatic's break for Germany after the Battle of Coronel. As I have argued, much was at stake, particularly in the North Sea. Reinforced by two heavy cruisers that—as the near destruction of HMS *Invincible* on December 8th showed—could inflict great harm on enemy battle cruisers, the Kaiser's navy had a greater chance of defeating Britain's pared down Grand Fleet. The High Seas Fleet deployed SMS *Blücher*, an upscale version of Graf Spee's armored cruisers, with its four battle cruisers, so his return would have tripled this wing of the scouting squadron and given it the best gunners in the world.

In discussing the squadron's attempt to reach home waters I emphasize one aspect of this last cruise that other historians have not—Graf Spee's gradually fading hope that dreadnoughts from the home fleet would reinforce him at sea. It is significant that aside from a brief mention in Tirpitz's memoirs the only printed word readers will find on Germany's Detached Division and its plans for a Flying Division as well as the former's cruise to South America under Prince Heinrich just months before war broke out are found in Graf Spee's posthumous memoirs assembled by Hermann Kirchoff, who had served in the East Asiatic Squadron, knew Graf Spee, and supported the Prince's controversial naval policies. Spee was also in the midst of these debates and discussions. Although admittedly a little speculative, it seems to me almost certain that while crossing the Pacific he must have had held out some hope for reinforcement by the Detached Division. And certainly he would have agreed with Schönberg's wish for ships "with more fighting power," which the arrival of SMS *Moltke* would have provided.[28]

Even without reinforcement, however, Graf Spee's dash for home was a closer run thing than other accounts reveal. What would have happened, for instance, if he had sailed for the Horn on November 4th rather than succumbing to his pessimistic nature and squandering eleven days? Would he have defeated Stoddart too and then eluded Sturdee? He did succumb to fatalism, of course, tragically transforming a

---

28   See Tirpitz, *My Memoirs*, 1:307; Kirchoff, *Maximilian Graf von Spee*, 25; and for the possibility of battle cruiser reinforcement of the East Asiatic, Geoffrey Bennett, *Naval Battles of the First World War* (New York, 1968), 103; and Maxwell Mulholland, formerly professor at the German Naval War College, "Potential Raids by German Battle Cruisers," in the website of *WWI-WWW: The War at Sea* (**www.gwpda.org/naval/ignbcrdr.htm**).

less-likely into a more-likely fate, but considering hypo-thetical alternatives is a way to measure the signifi-cance of his failings.

Furthermore, if Sturdee had been "Copenha-gened" at Port Stanley, "mauled at anchor" with Graf Spee stealing away to load coal off South America and disappearing into the huge spaces of the Atlantic Ocean, what then? And, as it turned out in the actual Battle of the Falklands, Graf Spee came much closer to winning than other historians realize. If either the action that did not occur in Port Stanley or the actual after-noon battle at sea had brought Spee another smash-ing victory, what then?

Obviously a lot of this is speculative, but none of it is idle speculation. To repeat, considering hypothetical alternatives sheds light on what was at stake in 1914 and measures the significance of what actually hap-pened. The First Lord of the Admiralty did not underes-timate the significance—and the risks—of sinking the German East Asiatic—and neither should historians. Even decades later, with the world mired in a second great war, Churchill did not consider the saga of Graf Spee's squadron an obscure side show of World War One—and neither should we.

CPSIA information can be obtained
at www.ICGtesting.com
Printed in the USA
BVHW01s1526230818
525302BV00042B/590/P